Pitt Press Series

T0352032

CHAUCER

THE PRIORESS'S TALE
THE TALE OF SIR THOPAS

CHAUCER

THE PRIORESS'S TALE
THE TALE OF SIR THOPAS

EDITED BY

LILIAN WINSTANLEY, M.A.

Lecturer in English in the University College
of Wales, Aberystwyth

CAMBRIDGE

AT THE UNIVERSITY PRESS

1922

CAMBRIDGE UNIVERSITY PRESS
Cambridge, New York, Melbourne, Madrid, Cape Town,
Singapore, São Paulo, Delhi, Tokyo, Mexico City

Cambridge University Press
The Edinburgh Building, Cambridge CB2 8RU, UK

Published in the United States of America by
Cambridge University Press, New York

www.cambridge.org
Information on this title: www.cambridge.org/9780521232968

First published 1922
First paperback edition 2011

A catalogue record for this publication is available from the British Library

ISBN 978-0-521-23296-8 Paperback

PREFACE

THE original research in this little book is to be found mainly in the Introduction to *Sir Thopas*. I believe there is still a great deal to be done in explaining the relation between the poetry of Chaucer and the historical and social conditions of his age; some hints of how these may affect the *Hous of Fame* and the *Knight's Tale* are given in Parts I and II, but in the case of *Sir Thopas* I have attempted to work it out in detail.

I trust the result may be of general interest to scholars.

LILIAN WINSTANLEY.

1 *June*, 1922.

CONTENTS

INTRODUCTION

I

CHAUCER AND HIS AGE

THE life of Chaucer, as generally computed, covers the years from 1340 to 1400; the latter half of the 14th century.

He is acknowledged as the father of English poetry; Spenser, himself the first of the great Elizabethans, reverenced Chaucer as his chief teacher in the English tongue and, in attempting to complete the unfinished *Squire's Tale*, invokes him as the most 'renowned poet':

> 'Thy pardon O most sacred happie spirit,
> That I thy labours lost may thus revive.'

Most of Spenser's successors have hailed him as the morning star of our poetry. Chaucer was also the first English poet to bring English literature into close and vital connection with the great literatures of France and Italy.

Anglo-Saxon had produced a literature of its own, one really powerful and vigorous considering the period (7th to 9th centuries); but it was interrupted by the Danes who swept away Northumbrian learning and Northumbrian poetry and, as Alfred shows, almost destroyed the whole work of culture in the land; Alfred himself helped to revive a West Saxon literature, mainly in prose, and to preserve piously the older memorials.

The Norman Conquest of 1066 introduced French literature as the standard form and, for several centuries, the writers of the fashionable world composed in French; Anglo-French flourished greatly; English literature proper became provincial in its method and outlook. We possess a considerable number of English poems, composed between the Conquest and the age of Chaucer; but they are, for the most part, uncertain in metre and style. The influence of French becomes stronger as time proceeds; there is a larger admixture of French words in the vocabulary and a greater tendency to the French method of versification; much Middle-English verse is a confusing mixture of the Anglo-Saxon alliterative and accentual type with the French type—syllabic and rhymed. The subject-matter also becomes more cosmopolitan; French themes are often chosen and there is a tendency to turn to the great international cycles of Alexander, Charlemagne and Troy.

Chaucer's attitude towards these different cycles varies greatly. For the tale of Troy he always expresses unbounded reverence—in the *Hous of Fame, Troilus and Criseyde*, etc.; the legends of Alexander and Charlemagne he respects; but he does not, except in briefest fashion, allude to them, while the Arthurian cycle he is inclined to refer to with contempt.

The truth is that in this, as in so many other respects, Chaucer belongs to the main stream of European thought and is not insular. The tale of Troy concerned the origins of both Rome and Britain; Virgil and Geoffrey of Monmouth and many others narrated how fugitives from Troy had laid the foundations of Western civilisation and Chaucer is concerned with that legendary material which binds England to the Continental system rather than with that which differentiates it.

A really great poet can scarcely be produced except in a great age. However original a man's genius may be, he requires a vigorous and powerful society to provide him with his material and a genuine breath of inspiration to kindle him into flame. Chaucer, though he seems from our distance to stand so much alone, was, in reality, the product of such a distinguished age and was himself only the most eminent among numerous contemporaries.

The 14th century was a period of revival both in England and on the Continent. The first breath of the Renaissance was already kindling Italy and France; the arts were reviving; great political and social changes were taking place and great religious changes were rapidly becoming inevitable. It was an age of unrest and upheaval but also of fresh, vigorous and abounding life. Even by Chaucer's time Italy had produced a number of gifted painters, sculptors and architects; among painters we may mention Cimabue and Giotto, Simone Martini, Memmi and Taddeo Gaddi; among sculptors and architects Niccolo and Giovanni Pisani, Giotto, Andrea Pisano and Andrea Orcagna.

Chaucer, on his Italian journeys, must have seen many of these artistic achievements and his passionate love for painting and sculpture is revealed in many portions of his work, particularly in the gorgeous temples described in the *Knight's Tale*.

There is, for instance, the representation of Venus:

> 'The statue of Venus, glorious for to see,
> Was naked fleting in the large see,
> And fro the navele down all covered was
> With wawes grene, and brighte as any glas.
> A citole in hir right hand hadde she,
> And on hir heed, ful semely for to see,
> A rose garland, fresh and wel smellinge,
> Above hir heed hir dowves flikeringe.'

And of Diana:

> 'This goddesse on an hert ful hye seet,
> With smale houndes al aboute hir feet,
> And undernethe hir feet she hadde a mone,
> Wexing it was and sholde wanie sone.
> In gaude grene hir statue clothed was
> With bowe in hand and arwes in a cas.'

It is impossible to come across such descriptions without seeing the close resemblance between them and the early mythological paintings of Italy, such, for instance, as those in the palaces of Ferrara.

Chaucer's Theseus has the same zest and eagerness in patronising art as that shown by the Italian nobles or as the poet's own patron—John of Gaunt—who was famous for the magnificence of his buildings:

> 'For in the land there nas no crafty man,
> That geometrie or ars-metrik can,
> Ne purtreyour, ne kerver of images,
> That Theseus ne yaf him mete and wages,
> The theatre for to maken and devyse.'

In literature Italian achievement was the greatest in the modern world; in the generation before Chaucer, Italy had produced in Dante the first modern to rival the supreme glory of Virgil; Petrarch and Boccaccio were Chaucer's own contemporaries.

The study of Greek was commencing, though only just commencing, for it was not until the middle of the next century that the fall of Constantinople scattered the Greek scholars over Europe and made Greek learning generally accessible. In the person of Petrarch poetry received greater honour than it had received even in the age of the troubadours and Chaucer is certainly thinking of his public crowning when he alludes to him as 'the laureate poete.' Everywhere learning increased in importance; great libraries and universities were being founded, great princes became patrons of learning and in many of the Italian cities—Verona, Ferrara, Rimini and Urbino—there flourished those Italian courts which were nurturing a new kind of life, the life of the courtier who was at once a man of affairs, a soldier, a diplomat, a scholar, a musician and a poet.

It was a life singularly varied and many sided; its full flower was described in a later age in the *Courtier* of Castiglione, but the ideal itself was already alive in Chaucer's day and Chaucer himself was no mean example of it; at different times in his life he was page and squire and soldier, courtier and diplomat, scholar and astronomer and, throughout all, the accomplished and eloquent poet.

Chaucer travelled in France, Flanders and Italy; he knew all three well and how much he owed to them is abundantly evident in his work. There is no poet who

reveals a more exquisite delight in the cunning of the
human hand, none for whom the arts of civilisation
are things more marvellous and more full of delight
or whose reverence for learning is more touching and
complete.

A scholar in the Miltonic sense he never could have
been—his ideal in life was too many-sided and too varied
—but no one has spoken more exquisitely of the scholar's
life. In the Clerk of Oxford he gives us the very spirit of
those early universities, Bologna and Paris, Oxford and
Cambridge, of which mediaeval Europe was so justly
proud. Oxford was, in Chaucer's time, a great centre of
vigorous intellectual life; for many years Wyclif lived
and taught there, instructing a chosen band of disciples
in his religious propaganda. Fourteenth-century Oxford
stood for freedom of thought and for intellectual liberty
as against the tyranny of Rome; it was already fighting
the same battle which Cambridge fought so magnificently
two centuries later. That Chaucer was well in the van of
his age, that he too was a passionate lover of freedom of
thought, there is abundant evidence to show, and he has
given us in this portrait of the Clerk the most delicate
tribute to Wyclif's university. The Clerk lives hard and
sparely; he loves the volumes of Aristotle more than
rich garments or musical instruments; he lives on the
gifts of patrons and gladly prays for the souls of those
who give him 'wherewith to scoleye.' So lovingly is the
portrait drawn that many have seen in it an image of
Chaucer in his own youth. This is very possible, the more
so as Chaucer makes him claim a journey to Italy and a
meeting with Petrarch which were, we may be fairly sure,
the poet's own experience. There is no evidence, however,
that Chaucer went to either university and the prob-
abilities are all against it. What is certain is that he
availed himself zealously of his opportunities and was,
for that age, a well-read and even a learned man. He did
not know Greek but there were very few in Europe
who did and Chaucer humorously acknowledges his own
ignorance:

> 'But the Troyane gestes, as they felle
> In Omer, or in Dares or in Dyte,
> Who-so that can, may rede hem as they wryte[1].'

He was, however, well read in the Latin authors available for his time; he himself names among his exemplars:

> 'Virgil, Ovyde, Lucan and Stace';

he translated Boëthius and to this list must be added at any rate Cicero and Seneca. It is obvious that he studies the Latin poets far more deeply and with increased seriousness after his visits to Italy; the curious manner in which both Virgil and Dante are made prominent in the *Hous of Fame* suggests that Dante had led him, as would be natural enough, to a fresh and yet more reverent study of Virgil.

Chaucer was also well read in mediaeval Latin; the *Wyf of Bath's* 'Prologue' and the *Nonnë Prestes Tale* in particular mention a number of curious and out-of-the-way authors such as Nigellus Wereker, St Jerome, Dionysius Cato, Geoffrey de Vinsauf, etc. Chaucer seems to have understood how exceedingly quaint many of these authors really were; they appealed to his unrivalled sense of humour.

Chaucer's references to classical mythology are often somewhat strange; they are the references of a man who had to rely mainly on his memory and who had no large library at hand for reference; but they serve to show what was, for the time, a considerable breadth of knowledge. The forms of the proper names occasionally suggest that he was taking them at second hand from some Italian author; Chaucer does indeed perceive his classical world from almost precisely the same angle of view as the Italian primitives; it is a world full of joy and freshness, regarded with intense reverence; but also with a quaint mediaeval formalism.

Chaucer was well read in both French and Italian. The French poem which he knew best seems to have been the great mediaeval allegory of the *Roman de la Rose*; he

---

[1] *Troilus and Criseyde*, I. 21.

translated, at any rate, a portion of this (he himself says
'all') and he very frequently quotes from and imitates it.

He was also acquainted with a number of French poets
forgotten to-day; such as de Deguilevile, Machault, de
Gransoun and Deschamps. An eminent French critic[1]
has, however, pointed out that Chaucer's knowledge of
mediaeval French does not include many of its best
things. He did not know the finest of the old 'trouvères'
or the most primitive saint legends which are also the
noblest:

'Même parmi les romans en vers, les plus beaux lui échap-
pèrent; rien ne permet de supposer qu'il ait connu Chrestien
de Troyes.'

Chaucer may have known Froissart personally and he
was almost certainly acquainted with his works; in many
respects his view of life agrees very closely with that of
Froissart; they were both lovers of chivalry, idealisers of
knightly virtues and knightly deeds, admirers of art and
pageantry and splendid tournaments; Chaucer is antago-
nistic to the democratic movements of the time and
Froissart actively and vehemently hostile· of all his
French contemporaries Chaucer was probably nearest to
Froissart in spirit and, as Gray has pointed out in an
illuminating passage[2], the intense interest in human life,
the rich abundance of human character, is the same both
in Chaucer and in the great French chronicler.

Italian writers taught Chaucer even more than the
Frenchmen. They taught him the art of great construction in poetry, the noble planning of work; they taught
him the use of an exquisitely wrought, delicate and subtle
style; they taught him keenness of analysis and psycho-
logical study of passion; they gave him models of admirable narrative—at once adequate and terse, full but
never verbose, perfectly arresting the reader's attention.

Chaucer refers to Dante with humility and reverence;
he gives many quotations from him especially in the *Hous*

[1] Légouis, *Chaucer*.
[2] *Letters*.

of Fame, and one of the tragedies in the *Monk's Tale* (that of Ugo) is taken from Dante's *Inferno*.

Petrarch also was greatly admired by Chaucer and his Clerk of Oxford claims to have learnt the tale of Griselda at Padua from Petrarch himself:

> 'whose rethoryke sweete
> Enlumined al Itaille of poetrye.'

Petrarch had set the example for all Europe of a fine and subtle analysis of the passion of love and this method Chaucer employs in *Troilus and Criseyde*; Boccaccio is his immediate source for the story; but, in the nobler type of the love described, in the reverence with which the character of the heroine is moulded and in the delicate fineness of the analysis Chaucer more nearly resembles Petrarch.

Boccaccio was, however, the Italian author from whom Chaucer borrowed most; curiously enough he never refers to him by name nor is there any proof that he was acquainted with Boccaccio's chief work—the *Decameron*; the latter did not, however, stand out as prominently for the men of the 14th century as it does for the modern world; Boccaccio's own age seems to have admired him as a poet rather than as a prose-writer, and Chaucer, himself a poet, naturally approached his genius from that side; *Troilus and Criseyde* and the *Knight's Tale* are adaptations from Boccaccio, taken respectively from the *Filostrato* and the *Teseide*.

The writers whom Chaucer reverenced most as personalities were undoubtedly Virgil and Dante—by far the greatest available in his age; but he owed more of his subject-matter to Boccaccio and Ovid; these, indeed, have talents more essentially akin to his own; they are among the world's greatest 'raconteurs'; they are almost unrivalled as narrative writers pure and simple and that also was Chaucer's supreme gift.

Chaucer, it should be observed, had in him the making of a man of science and his interest in science is also a sign of the Renaissance; he was well acquainted with astronomy and wrote a treatise on the use of the Astrolabe; he employs astronomical references to give notes of time and they are generally exact and careful.

It is, again, the keenly critical spirit of the early Renaissance that makes Chaucer so contemptuous in his attitude towards the superstitions of his day; they serve him mainly as matter for mirth; no one can miss the irony with which the practice of astrology is treated in his account of the 'Doctour of Phisyk'; he is bitter and contemptuous in his exposure of alchemy, even more bitter and contemptuous in his mockery at the false relics of the Pardoner; he ridicules the art of divining by dreams; he mocks at the eccentricities of mediaeval medicine.

Chaucer, we may take it then, was, at any rate so far as the arts and sciences were concerned, well in the main stream of European thought; it would not be true, as we shall see later, to say the same of his politics but it was certainly true of his attitude to art; he had a passionate love of its newly awakening power, alike in painting, in sculpture and in literature; he shared the desire of his age for knowledge; he had its enquiring, sceptical, scientific temper.

Let us next enquire how Chaucer is related to the great national and social movements of his day.

The latter half of the 14th century was a most interesting and significant period in English history. The reign of Edward III was marked by the brilliant victories gained over France at Crecy and Poictiers, by successes won against Scotland; England had two captive kings—John of France and Robert Bruce—at one time within her borders; English chivalry was famous throughout the world for its success and valour and the nobles and the middle classes were enriched by the magnificent spoil of the French cities.

At the same time the period had its gloomy and terrible aspects. In 1348–9 the Black Death carried off nearly half the population and it re-visited England five times before the close of the century. The greatest of these pestilences swept the country in Chaucer's childhood when he was too young to realise its horror; but the others must have swept away many of his friends and patrons. The *Pardoner's Tale* contains a most powerful picture of such a plague.

Arising largely out of the conditions created by the Black Death were the great labour problems which convulsed Europe; every country had its share of these and in England they culminated in the Peasants' Rebellion of 1381. Throughout western Europe there was a conflict not only between the peasants and the remainder of society, a revolt of the agricultural labourer; but there was also a struggle between the bourgeoisie of the towns and the feudal nobility; great cities like Ghent and Bruges, Lyons, Paris and London became conscious of their civic dignity; they sought independence and were often in revolt against their feudal superiors; in Flanders the latter portion of the 14th century was the age of the Arteveldes; it marks a bitter and prolonged class struggle of citizen against noble. The same phenomenon reappears in Paris where the citizens found a leader in Étienne Marcel and in England in the prolonged Parliamentary struggle. The 14th century is one of the most important periods in our English constitutional history. The western world was working out an enormous advance in political development. Now what was Chaucer's attitude to all this?

We must answer with candid truth. Chaucer, like Froissart, is almost entirely on the side of the feudal reaction. Chaucer's contemporary—Langland—seems to have been, in a quite special way, the poet of the common people and *Piers Plowman* mirrors for us all the burning political questions of the age; it discusses the labour troubles, the true position of the labourer; it considers the power of Parliament and reveals plainly the growing importance of the Commons.

There is nothing of this in Chaucer; he never mentions Parliaments except quite conventionally or in irony; the *Parlement of Foules* with the absurd speeches of the waterfowl—the ducks and geese—might have been intended as a satire on the Commons, quite possibly it was.

Chaucer, with naïve anachronism, introduces a Parliament into *Troilus and Criseyde*; but it gives bad advice and brings about the ruin of Troy; his references to the common people are not numerous and are almost invariably unsympathetic; we have the famous outburst in the *Clerk's Tale*:

> 'O stormy people, unsad and ever untrewe,
> Aye indiscreet and changing as a vane,
> Delighting ever in rumbel that is new,
> Brimful of clapping, dear ynogh a jane.'

And we have the ironical reference to the peasants' revolt in the *Nonnë Prestes Tale*:

> 'So hydous was the noyse, a benedicite!
> Certes, he Jakke Straw, and his meynee,
> Ne made nevere shoutes half so shrille
> Whan that they wolden any Flemyng kille.'

We know that, as a matter of fact, Chaucer's chief patron—John of Gaunt—was the head of the feudal reaction; he was the great champion of the aristocratic party and Chaucer takes almost inevitably his point of view. This is evident as soon as we consider the type of character which he chiefly admires and the sort of subjects which interest him most.

There is no more ideal character in the *Canterbury Tales* than that of the Knight; there is none treated with a sympathy more living; but this chivalrous ideal was emphatically that of the House of Lancaster.

Henry of Lancaster had been a famous crusader, alike in the Holy Land and in Prussia; John of Gaunt was more proud of his knighthood than of his estates, and Henry, Earl of Derby, afterwards Henry IV, distinguished himself by his passion for crusades. Walsingham tells us that in 1390 he conquered the army of the king of Lettow (Lithuania) taking prisoner four dukes and killing three.

In 1392 Capgrave gives a detailed account of Henry's journey through Europe to Jerusalem and back.

Henry was famous, the Christian world over, for his prowess in tournaments and gave several which were attended by knights from all parts of Europe. Chaucer himself, as Clerk of the Works, would have to make arrangements for the great tournament of 1390.

When Henry found himself able to force the crown from Richard II one of the great sources of his popularity lay in his fame as a crusader and a knightly champion and men contrasted his passion for noble adventure with what they deemed the lethargy and supineness of Richard.

Another chivalrous picture, drawn with romantic beauty, is the delightful figure of the Squire with his passion for song and music, his ardour in love and his desire for adventure in his lady's service.

The Franklin, apparently a typical Parliamentarian, admires the Squire with all his heart as a pattern his own son will never rival and speaks with wistful regret of his son's inferiority.

Chaucer's two longest and most ambitious poems, the *Troilus and Criseyde* and the *Knight's Tale* are both stories of the chivalrous ideal.

His portraiture of women has the same bias; it would be impossible to find figures drawn with greater tenderness and reverence than the portraits of his grand dames: Blanche of Lancaster (*Book of the Duchesse*) and Anne of Bohemia (*Legend of Good Women*); we may add Canace in the *Squire's Tale* and Emily in the *Knight's Tale*.

When we turn, however, to the middle classes and the bourgeoisie we discover a sharp contrast in the method of portraiture. Chaucer quite frankly detests the bourgeoisie; he can give us admirable portraits of the poorest class of all—the ploughman and his brother—but the commercial money-making middle class he scorns. The Man of Lawe, Chaucer tells us, is of 'greet reverence' and then adds immediately 'He semed such, his wordes weren so wyse,' while the Doctour is plainly a charlatan.

The lower middle class Chaucer regards as being essentially dishonest; like the Reve and the Manciple they rob their employers whenever they get the chance, betraying all those who trust in them with cynical impudence; they all (and here Chaucer's testimony is at one with Langland's) treat cruelly the poor who fall into their power; the Miller steals flour and takes thrice his dues and yet is honest as millers go; the farm-bailiff and labourers were afraid of the Reeve 'as of the deeth,' and the Shipman is the worst of all for he plays pirate whenever he gets the chance and drowns the crew of any ship he takes:

> 'By water he sent hem hoom to every land.'

Another hint in the same direction is that Chaucer nowhere speaks against France. The knightly order throughout Europe regarded themselves as a unity and knew comparatively little of international bitterness; Froissart's sympathies are, quite obviously, more on the side of the plundering English nobles than of the oppressed and miserable French peasants. Chaucer's contemporary—Laurence Minot—who is much more a voice of the common people makes game of the ignominious defeat of the French king and his noblesse; but there is no hint of such bitterness in Chaucer.

On the whole his sympathies were emphatically with the aristocratic class and their ideals—their passion for art, for beauty of dress, beauty of gardens, their love of adventure, tournaments and chivalry, the whole romantic and splendid ideal of life which we find depicted in the pages of Froissart.

It remains to enquire concerning his attitude towards religion.

Chaucer's patron—John of Gaunt—was a patron of Wyclif and defended and maintained him against his enemies. Gaunt's support of Wyclif was, however, largely due to political reasons; Wyclif believed in apostolic purity; he inveighed against the luxury of the higher clergy and he disliked their interference in secular affairs. John of Gaunt, as the leader of the feudal party, was also jealous of the clergy because their occupation of secular offices came into conflict with the power of the

nobles. Therefore he gave his support to the great reformer.

There can be no doubt that Chaucer also espoused ardently the cause of Wyclif. As we have seen he gives us
a fascinating picture of the Clerk of Oxford, the university
which, under Wyclif's guidance, was struggling hard for
freedom of thought; the Church ultimately conquered
and suppressed that freedom; but Chaucer certainly reveals his sympathy with the disinterested ideals of the
university; the portrait shows also that simplicity and
poverty of life which was a part of the Wyclifite ideal
alike for the men of learning and the men of religion.

Wyclif's philosophical ideas are, quite plainly, just
those philosophical ideas which interested Chaucer most.
Wyclif commenced his career as a theologian by following up the great Augustinian controversy started by
Thomas afterwards Bishop Bradwardine, on the subject
of predestination *versus* free-will. Wyclif finally arrived
at a belief in predestination, in this as in so many other
respects anticipating the Calvinistic reformers of a later
date.

Now the question of free-will *versus* predestination was
Chaucer's favourite philosophical problem and references
to it are continually cropping up in his works as in the
Nonnë Prestes Tale:

> 'But what that God forwoot moot nedes bee,
> After the opinion of certain clerkis.
> Witnesse on hym that any parfit clerk is,
> That in scole is greet altercacion
> In this mateere, and greet disputison
> And hath been of an hundred thousand men.'

Then Chaucer refers to the chief philosophical authori-
ties who have discussed the problem: Augustine, Boëthius,
Bishop Bradwardine:

> 'Whether that Goddes worthy forwityng
> Streyneth me nedely for to doon a thyng;
> Or elles if free choys be graunted me
> To do that same thing or do it noght.'

Wyclif was a life-long opponent of Rome, of what he believed its corruption and its tyranny; he objected especially to the jurisdiction of the ecclesiastical courts.

So Chaucer also represents as among his very worst rogues the Pardoner and the Summoner; the Pardoner is the most skilful and dangerous of all his scoundrels; he has his wallet:

'Bret-ful of pardons, come from Rome al hoot,'

and there is no more drastic exposure in Chaucer's pages than the exposure of his trickeries. Wyclif, in this anticipating Luther, detested 'indulgences,' for he regarded the whole system as sapping the moral character of the people and, in the *Pardoner's* 'Prologue,' Chaucer makes his rogue explain with unbridled effrontery how the sale of such indulgences is carried on. Wyclif also preached against the worship of relics as a degrading form of superstition, and Chaucer tells of the glass crammed full of 'pigges bones.'

Wyclif, during one portion of his career, met with a great deal of sympathy from the mendicant friars whose ideal of the religious life did, indeed, in its conception agree with his own; but he also preached unsparingly against their corruptions, saying that they had become idle and mischievous, careless in their methods of dealing with the sins of the laity, giving short shrift and swift absolution; Chaucer presents us with the portrait of the 'limitour' in which all these traits are depicted with matchless skill:

'Ful swetely herde he confessioun
And plesaunt was his absolucioun.'

Wyclif, again, disbelieved in excommunication, he defied its power when it was uttered against himself and he doubted Rome's powers of absolution; Chaucer jests at both:

'For curs will slee right as assoiling saveth.'

Wyclif pointed out the many shortcomings and failings of the parish priests and founded his own order of 'poor priests' to show what such men should be. The same ideal is plainly expressed in Chaucer's 'Poor Persoun of a Toun'; everywhere in his portrait we see the poet contrasting him with the careless type which was common; he does *not* 'cursen for his tithes'; he does *not* leave his flock 'encombred in the myre' and go to London to seek a chantry. If we had any doubt about the identification it would be removed by the host—Hary Bailly—who accuses the 'Persoun' of being a Lollard which the latter does not even attempt to deny.

As the schism widened between Wyclif and the Church the great reformer turned more and more to the poor and unlearned and preached mainly to them and Chaucer represents the Plowman, the brother of the poor Persoun, as being one of the most ideal characters among his pilgrims; this character is doubtless derived directly from Langland's *Piers Plowman*.

Chaucer's age, as has already been said, was one of literary revival. There were several different dialects and the writers of each region employed their own dialect for purposes of composition. The Northern dialect was employed by two important writers, one on the Scottish and one on the English side of the Border. Barbour's *Bruce* (dated about 1345) is a fine patriotic poem; it is not historically accurate since it admits legend as freely as fact; but it gives a most noble and impassioned view of the heroic struggle of Scotland against Edward I. It reveals a magnificent love of liberty and its motto might be stated in its own words:

> 'A! fredome is a noble thing!
> Fredome all solace to man giffis;
> He levys at ease that frely levys.'

Servitude is more horrible than death, for it mars the whole man 'body and bones' while death 'annoys' him but once.

On the English side of the Border Laurence Minot was the most important writer; he was essentially a lyrical poet and he celebrates the victories of Edward III and the Black Prince in most vigorous style; his poems were probably contemporary with the different events they celebrate—Halidon Hill, Crecy, Sluys, etc.

Minot's poems are written in a somewhat rough metre: end-rhyme with a considerable amount of alliteration; they are powerful and stirring and full of strong contemporary prejudices against the French and Scotch. Minot's point of view, we may remark, was essentially a popular one.

The West Midland dialect had also a wide range; its northern variety occupied the country west of the Pennines in Lancashire and Cheshire; the population had probably a large admixture of Celtic blood and close connections with the Welsh across the Border; Arthurian subjects are more common in this region than elsewhere. The most remarkable of such works is the beautiful anonymous poem, written in alliterative measure, which is known as *Sir Gawayne and the Grene Knight*. Professor Gwynne Jones assures me he has little doubt that the poem is derived ultimately from a Welsh source; he thinks this proved by the forms of the proper names which occasionally show a definite mutation impossible except in Welsh and also by the Welsh forms of the place-names.

The genius of the Gawayne poet is closely akin to the romantic side of Chaucer's. The poem is a very beautiful romance of adventure and chivalry, full of delicacy, purity and true knightly feeling. It has affinities, in its gorgeous descriptive passages, with Chaucer's *Knight's Tale*; the portrait of Sir Gawayne in his armour may be set, in its superb splendour, side by side with the portraits of Emetreus and Lycurgus; the enchantments and marvels show affinity with the *Squire's Tale*; as a piece of mediaeval magic we may well compare the *Squire's Tale* with the opening of the Gawayne poem which tells how Arthur is holding his great yearly festival when an enchanter, clad all in green and riding upon a green horse, rides up to his board and challenges any of the knights present to exchange blows; all are silent, fearing his manifest strangeness and Arthur is about to take the challenge upon himself when Gawayne steps forth, accepts the conditions and strikes off at one blow the head of the stranger knight who proceeds to pick up his head, makes an appointment for a year and a day from that date and rides out with his head in his hand. Not even Chaucer could carry us more wonderfully to the heart of fairyland.

In the later portions of the poem which describe the trial of Gawayne's honour by the temptation of love we have a real subtlety of psychology. The Gawayne poet also has an unusually keen eye for colour and landscape; his description of North Wales in autumn and winter is one of the most rarely beautiful things in mediaeval literature. The whole tone of the poem is delicate and lofty and Gawayne, as a pattern of knightly honour and purity, can stand side by side with the noblest heroes of Spenser and Sidney.

In the same dialect and possibly by the same author is the beautiful elegy known as *The Pearl*; it consists of a series of lyrics, written in complex and elaborate stanza form, and lamenting the death of a girl of rare beauty, the daughter of the poet; the whole series has an exquisite graceful tenderness.

The southern variety of the West Midland dialect had its centre in Shropshire; its chief poet was William Langland known by his one poem of *Piers Plowman*. The poem was exceedingly popular in the 14th century, and we possess a great number of MSS.; it exists in three chief forms, usually known as the A, B and C texts and, from the literary point of view, the B text is by far the finest.

Piers Plowman is written in the Anglo-Saxon alliterative line; it may be founded upon a local legend of the Malvern Hills for the tale, that of a Plowman who is the guide and exemplar of man and who possesses superhuman strength and ultimately becomes a divine figure, is a tale found in folk-lore in many parts of Europe; it is found in the folk-lore of Russia, for instance, and the Malvern Hills really do mark the furthest point reached by a bronze age invasion coming from the Volhynian plain; we have the same tale in Scandinavian folk-lore[1].

[1] Heimskringla.

Piers Plowman is a long religious allegory divided into many separate versions. Langland represents the world as a place of pilgrimage where all men are seeking the truth and we may note incidentally that this possibly suggested to Chaucer the idea of a pilgrimage as his framework for the *Canterbury Tales*. Many false guides stand forth purporting to lead men to truth; the real guide is found in the shape of the Plowman—Piers—the hard-working, simple and unassuming man upon whose labour the whole foundation of society ultimately reposes.

Piers Plowman is the true Christian who suddenly becomes, by a stroke of great daring, the revelation of the divine in man—Christ Himself. Langland expresses most powerfully the social unrest as it existed in the 14th century; he is the voice of all that questioning, that sadness, that revolt which ultimately rose to the surface in the Peasants' Rebellion of 1381.

Langland gives us just that view of society which Chaucer does not; he is as much and as decidedly the voice of the people with their growing self-consciousness and power as Chaucer is the voice of the aristocratic and feudal reaction. We can see most plainly in Langland's pages the increasing importance of Parliament, the large part it already played in national life; Langland does not think it ought to be all-powerful; he conceives it as being for counsel rather than for command; he believes in a strong king who can lead his people, and the king and the Commons are together against the rest. Langland is deeply concerned with the inter-relations of the different orders of the State; he is no leveller; he believes in a hierarchy of ranks only he is sure that all other classes take advantage of the labourer, that his sufferings are cruel and his position unjust. We see the exact motives of the peasants' revolt.

Langland is not, like Chaucer, a devotee of the idea of chivalry; he shares Chaucer's view sufficiently to consider that the chivalrous orders are much better than the ecclesiastical and the knights altogether finer people than the monks and friars; but he perceives the unpractical side of the long pilgrimages and the religious tournaments; he shows the poor tenants at home squeezed for money to pay for these journeys, a prey to unscrupulous agents and victimised by the rapacity of highway robbers and bands of wandering marauders; the knight should put down such malefactors; but he is absent and the 'Roberds men' thrive.

In his picture of the religious orders Langland agrees closely with Chaucer; he shows the idleness of the monks and the nuns, the roguery of friars and summoners and the insolent effrontery of the pardoners and he adds, on account of their laziness, a bitter anger against hermits.

Chaucer, as we have seen, reveals the aristocrat's dislike of the bourgeoise class as mean people, always concerned with money-making and essentially dishonest. Langland has the poor man's dislike of them which is far more bitter and furious; he calls on the king and commons to make laws to punish severely the

'Brewsteres and baksters . bochers and cokes;
For thise aren men on this molde . þat most harme worcheth
To the pore peple that parcel-mele buggen.'

He tells us indignantly that they buy 'rentes'; they 'build high' by poisoning the food and pinching the bellies of the poor. A typical example of Langland's middle-class is the innkeeper who, on being told that 'restitution' would be proper for him, at once understands it to be the French word for robbery.

In Chaucer's own dialect there was one important contemporary writer—his personal friend—John Gower. Gower is typical of the confusion as to language which existed in fashionable circles for he wrote a long poem in Latin and one in French before turning to English. It was probably Chaucer's success which suggested to him the employment of English in his *Confessio Amantis*, which consists of a series of stories set in the framework provided by the confession of a lover. Gower is a good narrative writer; but he has not the romantic beauty of

the 'Gawayne' poet nor the passionate strength of Langland, far less the rich genius of Chaucer.

Interesting as are the other writers of the 14th century
Chaucer is, by far, the greatest English poet of his age.
He owed his achievement mainly to the fact that he per-
ceived far more plainly than his contemporaries the neces-
sity for true literary canons, for true artistic form and
greatness of conception and he turned to the literature
which had, at that time, more to offer than any other in
Europe. He learnt from the great Italians the secret of
noble construction and imperishable style, and it is
mainly by his style that he stands pre-eminent. His
English contemporaries have many virtues; but they
never catch that accent of the world's great poetry which,
when he has once learnt his art, comes so naturally and
so inevitably to Chaucer's lips.

No other English poet before him can show such lines
as:

> 'Singest with vois memorial in the shade
> Under the laurer which that may not fade[1],

or

> 'The smyler with the knyf under the cloke[2],'

or

> 'What is this world? what asketh men to have
> Now with his love, now in his colde grave,
> Alone withouten any compagnye?'

or

> 'Hyde ye youre beautés, Ysoude and Eleyne;
> My lady comith, that al this may disteyne.'

There is no mistaking the accent of such as these—their
high dignity, their easy mastery, their lingering haunting
beauty.

And Chaucer is no less a master of irony and humour
than of dignity and pathos; Chaucer's humour is everywhere; it is the magic atmosphere which seems to bathe
all his poetry as with sharp clear light. It is the main
secret of his incomparable vividness.

---

[1] *Anelida and Arcite.*   [2] *Knight's Tale.*

The circumstances of Chaucer's life were such as to bring him into contact with men and affairs and to take him frequently abroad. We know more of his life than of most mediaeval poets because he was engaged the greater part of his time in the public service and thus we are able to discover information in public records.

Geoffrey Chaucer was, by birth, a citizen of London. The family name appears to be of French origin and to mean 'shoemaker,' being originally the same as the Latin 'calcearius.' That this was the original meaning of the name is made more probable by the fact that the poet's father and grandfather lived first in Cordwainers' Street; the poet's father—John Chaucer—certainly became a vintner and it is probable that the grandfather—Robert le Chaucer—had previously chosen the same trade. In 1308 Robert le Chaucer was attorney to the King's Butler in the Port of London.

John Chaucer appears to have had some connection with the Royal Family, for in 1338 he went abroad in the king's retinue and was attendant upon the king and queen in their expeditions to Flanders and Cologne. In a City ordinance of 1342 John Chaucer is described as a vintner. His wife—Agnes—was niece of Nigel de Hackney, formerly of Hamo de Copton, and from him inherited property; both John and Agnes were of rank sufficient to bear arms as is shown by their seals; they each possessed property in various places such as Ipswich, Stepney and London.

Geoffrey Chaucer was a Londoner born and bred; but he appears to have been educated rather for a courtier than for the city. The date of the poet's birth is usually fixed about 1340; this is calculated mainly from his own evidence given in the Scrope and Grosvenor Trial of 1386 in which he states that he was then 'forty years of age and upwards' and had borne arms for twenty-seven years. All ages mentioned in the trial are given in round figures; but it is obvious that the date of 1340 may be somewhat too early.

The poet's father seems to have taken advantage of

his court connection to get his son placed in the employ of Elizabeth de Burgh, Countess of Ulster in her own right and the wife of Lionel, Duke of Clarence, Edward III's third son. In the household accounts of this lady we have records of a page's uniform given to Geoffrey Chaucer. It is interesting to observe that we also have records of payments made to a certain Philippa Pan (*i.e.* Panetaria or Lady of the Pantry) who may be identical with the Philippa whom Chaucer afterwards married.

All his life the poet had many opportunities of travel, and they must certainly have commenced when he was in attendance upon the Countess of Ulster for she visited Windsor, Woodstock, Doncaster, Hatfield in Yorkshire, Anglesey, etc.

In the year 1359, as we learn from his own deposition in the Scrope and Grosvenor Trial, Chaucer took part in the military expedition to France; he states that he was armed as an 'esquire'; the usual age for military service was about nineteen so this would agree with the date already suggested for his birth in 1340. Chaucer was taken prisoner, but ransomed on March 1st, 1360, when the king paid £16 towards the ransom, though whether this was the whole sum or a portion only we have no means of knowing.

It was not the custom to treat prisoners of war with great severity and Chaucer's early work shows such a keen appreciation of French literature that the time of his imprisonment may have been one of real value for his intellectual development. Professor Skeat believes that, during his period of military service, he may still have been in Duke Lionel's retinue.

Chaucer was probably in the king's service from 1360 to 1366 as in the latter year he received an annuity from the king. In 1366 also we find him married to a lady named Philippa whose surname is, however, only a matter of conjecture. Chaucer's wife certainly had some important and intimate connection with the household of John of Gaunt and it is obvious, from several circumstances, that her influence at Court was greater than his

own and it was probably through her instrumentality
that the poet obtained the life-long and most valuable
patronage of John of Gaunt.

It has been conjectured that Philippa may have been
the daughter of Sir Payne Roet, Guienne King of Arms
and sister to Katharine Swynford who was, for a long
time, the mistress and afterwards became the third wife
of John of Gaunt; on the other hand it is possible that
she was related to Sir Hugh de Swynford, Katharine's
first husband. In the year 1366 Philippa Chaucer received a pension from the king though she is not then
mentioned definitely as being the wife of Geoffrey; the
payment was to continue for life or until the king should
make other provision 'for her estate.'

In 1367 the king granted an annuity of twenty marks
to his 'beloved Yeoman' Geoffrey Chaucer and the payments were continued, though with some irregularities,
until 1389; Chaucer is termed indifferently 'Yeoman' and
'Esquire.' His duties in the royal household would be of
a somewhat menial character such as carving, carrying
torches, etc.; they were such as were in that age esteemed
honourable.

In June 1370 Chaucer went abroad with royal letters
of protection.

In Nov. 1372 Chaucer was commissioned with two
others to treat with the Doge and citizens of Genoa for
the establishment of a market in some place on the English coast to which the Genoese merchants might resort
with their goods. In May 1373 he returned to London,
his accounts showing that he had both men and horses
in his train; he states that he had visited Florence and,
as previously explained, he probably met Petrarch who
was residing at Arqua near Padua from 1370 to 1374.

This was Chaucer's first journey to Italy; his experience of that country plays, as we have seen, an immense
part in his life though its influence probably did not reach
its height until after his second journey.

In April 1374 the king granted Chaucer a pitcher
of wine daily and in the same year the poet took a

lease of a house at Aldgate from the Corporation of London.

Soon after, in June 1374, Chaucer obtained a patent appointing him Controller of the Customs and Subsidy of wools, hides and wool-fells in the Port of London on condition that he should write his rolls with his own hand and personally dwell there and perform the duties without any substitute. This was a very important post for the wool trade was the main export of the 14th century; the wool was conveyed to Flanders to be made into cloth, and the wool customs were one of the chief sources of the king's revenue. The post was of considerable monetary value and considered very honourable; it was usually given to some prominent citizen.

Chaucer took his oath as Controller in June 1374, and the next day at the Savoy John of Gaunt granted him an annuity of £10 for life as a reward for his services to the Duke and for those of his wife—Philippa—to the Duke's consort—Blanche. This is the first document which directly mentions Philippa as the wife of Geoffrey; judging from the fact that her pensions both from the king, and from the duke, were granted before his own, it seems obvious that she possessed more favour at Court.

In 1375 Chaucer received two Kentish wardships, one of Edmund Staplegate and one of John de Solys; guardians were well paid for their duties to their wards and such grants were therefore of considerable value.

In 1376 Chaucer was sent abroad 'on the king's secret affairs' and in 1377 in company with Sir Thomas de Percy he was despatched to Flanders 'on the king's secret affairs.'

In June 1377 the new king—Richard II—confirmed Chaucer in his office as 'Controller of Wool Customs,' and he remained in the royal service as an 'esquire.'

In 1378 a marriage was projected between Richard II and a French princess and Chaucer was among the commissioners sent to France.

In May 1378 Chaucer visited Lombardy in the retinue of Sir Edward de Berkeley on a mission to the Lord of

Milan (Bernabo Visconti) and Sir John Hawkwood. Chaucer left London in May and returned in September. It is after this second journey that the Italian influence in his work becomes most plainly evident.

In 1379 and 1380 Geoffrey and Philippa were still receiving their annuities from John of Gaunt. Philippa is styled by the Duke 'nostre chere et bien amee Damoiselle'; she was apparently in attendance on the Duke's second wife—Constance of Castile.

On April 20th, 1382, Chaucer obtained the office of Controller of the Petty Customs in the Port of London. A second patent was made out to him on May 8th, empowering him 'to exercise the office' by himself or 'his sufficient deputy for whom he would be willing to answer,' this privilege was a great and unusual favour.

In Feb. 1385 Chaucer petitioned the king for leave to appoint a permanent deputy 'at the Wool-quay' and the king granted his prayer. He was now free from the personal attendance which he had been compelled to make for more than ten years, ever since June 1374.

Chaucer certainly had some important connection with Kent which may have been due to the fact that John of Gaunt possessed considerable property—the Manor of Eagle—in that county. On Oct. 12th, 1385, Chaucer was appointed Justice of the Peace for Kent; the patent 'associates' him with Simon Burley, Warden of the Cinque Ports, John de Cobham and other Kentish magnates. On June 28th, 1386, a commission was granted to him and other Justices, setting out their duties at full length.

In the same year—1386—Philippa Chaucer, Henry Earl of Derby, son of John of Gaunt, Sir Thomas de Swynford and six others were admitted into the fraternity of Lincoln Cathedral, John of Gaunt being present. This seems to show conclusively that Philippa was connected with the House of Lancaster and probably with the Swynford family. The brethren and sisters promised to assist and maintain the minster and were accordingly admitted 'in all prayers, fastings, pilgrimages, almsdeeds and works of mercy connected therewith.'

Edward III, the Black Prince, John of Gaunt, Richard II and his queen were all at various times admitted to this order. The Duke of Lancaster seems to have had an especial interest in Lincoln Cathedral, for he had inherited the important barony of Spalding or Bolingbroke in Lincolnshire.

In Aug. 1386 Chaucer was elected Knight of the Shire for Kent, probably following on his office of Justice of the Peace.

In Oct. 1386 Chaucer appeared in the Refectory of Westminster Abbey as a witness in the famous Scrope and Grosvenor Trial; it is from his evidence that we derive several of the most important facts in his life. This same year was a very crucial one for Chaucer, since his patron—John of Gaunt—went abroad on his ill-fated expedition to Spain, and Chaucer was deprived of his two valuable offices—the Controllerships. John of Gaunt remained in Spain 1386–9; the Duke of Gloucester came into power and all Gaunt's party were equally obnoxious to him. Gloucester's party had obtained a royal commission to enquire into abuses in the Customs and Subsidies and seem to have taken the opportunity of getting rid of Chaucer.

The last payment of Philippa Chaucer's pension was made June 18th, 1387, which was probably near the date of her death.

On May 1st, 1388, Chaucer petitioned that his pension of forty marks might be assigned to one John Scalby; the precise meaning of this transaction is doubtful; but it almost certainly signifies that he was in pecuniary difficulties.

Richard II, when he seized the reins, showed favour to Chaucer by appointing him Clerk of the King's Works on July 12th, 1389; the royal residences under his control included the Palace of Westminster, the Tower of London and the Manor of Shene. This was a more valuable post than his former Controllership.

In March 1390 he was made a commissioner to survey 'sewers, bridges, causeways, weirs and trenches,' with powers to compel landowners to make or repair such works 'between the towns of Greenwich and Woolwich.'

In May and Oct. 1390 it would be part of Chaucer's duty as Clerk of the Works to cause scaffolds to be erected for the jousts held in Smithfield before the King and Queen.

On July 12th, 1390, he was made Clerk of the Works at Windsor.

In 1390 or 1391 Chaucer was appointed Sub-Forester of the forest of North Petherton by Roger Mortimer, Earl of March, the chief forester.

In 1391 Chaucer lost his office of Clerk of the Works.

In Feb. 1394 the king granted him an annuity of £20 in consideration of the good service he had rendered. Some time between Feb. 1395 and Feb. 1396 Chaucer received £10 on behalf of Henry, Earl of Derby from the Clerk of the Earl's Great Wardrobe; this suggests that he was probably in personal attendance upon the Earl. In Dec. 1397 the king granted to Chaucer a butt or pipe of wine yearly in the Port of London.

In 1398 Chaucer applied for letters of protection which were granted and the application seems to suggest that he had enemies.

Henry IV gained possession of the throne in 1399. Chaucer was confirmed in his previous grant of twenty marks and received an annuity of fifty marks; but, probably owing to the new king's financial troubles, only a portion of his pensions appears to have been paid. The last payment made to him is dated June 5th, 1400.

According to the inscription on his tomb in Westminster Abbey Chaucer died Oct. 25th, 1400, probably in the house of which he was lessee close to the Abbey.

A certain wealthy individual—Thomas Chaucer—who played a prominent part in the Parliaments of Henry IV and Henry V is described by tradition as the poet's son. Some connection is certain for Thomas Chaucer held one of Geoffrey's offices—forester of North Petherton—under Henry V, and he also held the lease of Geoffrey's house at Westminster.

Of the poet's personality we have little knowledge, except what can be derived from his own writing. We have one good portrait which we owe to his disciple Occleve; it represents Chaucer, apparently in old age, and shows a face delicate and refined, almost wistful.

Chaucer's references to his own tastes and habits are few, and the most important occur in the *Hous of Fame* and the Prologue to the *Legend of Good Women*. In the former the eagle twits him with his intense devotion to study; after his labours in the counting-house he goes home and stupefies himself with another book:

> 'For whan thy labour doon al is,
> And hast y-maad thy rekeninges,
> In stede of rest and newe thinges,
> Thou goest hoom to thy house anoon;
> And, also doumb as any stoon,
> Thou sittest at another boke,
> Till fully daswed is thy loke.'

In the same passage the eagle observes that the poet is so completely absorbed in his own concerns that he hears nothing, even of his neighbours, and would live exactly like a hermit were it not for the fact that his abstinence is but little.

In the *Legend of Good Women* (the Prologue) he tells us that he holds books in very great reverence, he loves to read in them and nothing will draw him away except occasionally upon a holiday or when the month of May arrives:

> 'Whan that I here the smale foules singe,
> And that the floures ginne for to springe,
> Farwel my studie, as lasting that sesoun.'

The facts of Chaucer's life show us that he was, during by far the greater part, actively engaged in affairs and, under the circumstances, it must have needed an amazing amount of industry to leave so large a volume of work. It is not surprising that Chaucer is a poet of 'torsos' and that quite a number of his poems, including some of the very best—the *Legend of Good Women*, the *Squire's Tale*, etc.—were left unfinished.

Chaucer's continual contact with life helps to explain, no doubt, the reality of his work. Few poets can have known the world more widely. He was acquainted with kings and princes, probably in the case of John of Gaunt and Henry, Earl of Derby, quite intimately. His offices as Controller and Clerk of the Works must have brought him in contact, equally well, with the middle class, and his journeys abroad both widened his mind and taught him to see his own country more clearly, freshly and distinctly.

Chaucer has provided the reader with several lists of his works. In the Prologue to the *Legend* the god of love accuses Chaucer of having written poems which tend to disgust men with love such as the *Romaunt of the Rose*,

'That is an heresye ageyns my law,'

and also complains of *Troilus and Criseyde*. Alcestis, on the other hand, quotes many works which tend, either directly or indirectly, to the honour of women: the *Hous of Fame*, the *Dethe of Blaunche the Duchesse*, the *Parlement of Foules*, etc. There is another list in the Prologue to the *Man of Law's Tale* which deals mainly with the *Legend of Good Women* and its contents, though they do not tally with the poem as we possess it, and seem to show that Chaucer had contemplated an extension.

There is again a third list in the retractation appended to the *Canterbury Tales* in which the author expresses contrition for such of those tales as 'sounen unto sinne,' but claims credit for the rest. Lydgate, in the Prologue to his *Falls of Princes*, also gives a list of Chaucer's works.

From these four taken together a very reliable canon may be compiled, though it is evident that some works have disappeared such as the one which Chaucer calls the *Book of the Lion* or the one Lydgate terms *Daunt in Englyssh* which may, very possibly, have consisted of translations from Dante like the life of Ugo in the *Monk's Tale*. Some short pieces are also ascribed to Chaucer on very reliable MS. evidence.

Chaucer tells us that he translated the *Romaunt of the*

Rose; but the existing translation, traditionally ascribed to him, is both incomplete and inconsecutive; it falls into three distinct portions and differences of dialect and of technique suggest that the three may be by different authors; it is possible that only the first portion is Chaucer's. This is one of the most charming, sweet and gay of all Middle English poems, full of admirable pictures. Its delicate and refined portraits of women—allegorical figures—greatly influenced Spenser. We may quote a few lines to show how close their manner is to that of the *Faerie Queene*. Chaucer says of Ydelnesse:

> 'Hir face whyt and wel coloured,
> With litel mouth and round to see;
> A clove chin' eek hadde she.
>
> . . . .
>
> Hir throte also whyt of hewe
> As snow on braunche snowed newe.'

And of Fraunchyse:

> 'With eyen gladde, and browes bente;
> Hir heer down to hir heles wente.
> And she was simple as douve on tree,
> Ful debonaire of herte was she.'

In the Prologue to the *Legend* Alcestis mentions the poet as having composed many songs in honour of the god of love:

> 'And many an ympne for your halydayes,
> That highten Balades, Roundels, Virelayes.'

The works referred to were, in all probability, lyrical poems in the French fashion and the greater number must have perished as comparatively few survive; some of these such as *Merciles Beaute, a Triple Roundel, To Rosemounde, a Balade* are little more than metrical exercises.

On the other hand some of the later 'balades' whose subjects were taken from Boëthius are nobly beautiful and we have at least one exquisite specimen of the love 'balade'—that contained in the Prologue to the *Legend*:

> 'Hyd, Absolon, thy gilte tresses clere;
> Ester, lay thou thy meknesse al adoun.'

If many of Chaucer's lost songs equalled this then their disappearance must be regarded as one of the great misfortunes of English letters.

Chaucer's earliest original poem of any length appears to have been the *Book of the Duchesse* dated by its subject 1369. Here, though we find the poet essaying his strength, he only ventures upon brief flights, for he is still largely imitative; the poem is, in fact, almost a 'cento' compiled from different authors, such as the two poets of the *Roman de la Rose*, de Lorris and de Meung, Machault, etc.

The best thing it contains is the account of the Duchess herself whom Chaucer probably knew well. It is a noble portrait of a great lady, free from all envy, speaking no evil, full of sweet courtesy, loyal in all her deeds and invariably true:

> 'And I dar seyn and swere hit wel—
> That Trouthe him-self, over and al,
> Had chose his maner principal
> In hir that was his resting-place.'

It may be remarked that we have also the warrant of Froissart for the fact that Blanche of Lancaster was one of the noblest women of her age.

Chaucer's metre, in his earliest poems, is the octosyllabic couplet; after his journey to Italy in 1372 he was, however, impressed by the beauty of the Italian 'ottava rima' and for some time after his favourite metre is a seven-lined stanza somewhat similar but perhaps of even greater poetic value. Professor Saintsbury remarks that his pitching on it and his preference for it are alike proofs of his instinctive genius for prosody.

Chaucer experiments very beautifully with this metre in the *Parlement of Foules* and brings it to perfection in *Troilus and Criseyde*.

It is the custom to assign a certain number of the *Canterbury Tales*, the majority of those written in stanza, to this period (1372–86): the *Second Nun's Tale* of St Cecilia; the *Man of Law's Tale*—the story of Constance—the unhappy royal heroine who floats for 'years and days' upon the sea, all alone in a small boat without food or drink but sustained by divine power. Both these are obviously early work for they are very naïve and primitive.

The 'Clerk's' story of Griseldis may also belong to this period though, possibly, it was re-written for the *Canterbury Tales*; it is, at any rate, one of the most exquisite things that Chaucer ever wrought, all pathos and tenderness. To this period there certainly belongs some version of the *Knight's Tale*, for in the Prologue to the *Legend* Chaucer speaks of having written a work entitled *Al the love of Palamon and Arcite*; it is possible that the poem he alludes to is not the one we possess but an earlier version in stanza.

The independent works of this period are the *Parlement of Foules, Troilus and Criseyde* and the *Hous of Fame*. The first of these is dated by its subject 1382; it is a court piece written to celebrate a royal betrothal, almost certainly that of Richard II to Anne of Bohemia, for all the circumstances tally. There are reminiscences of the *Roman de la Rose*, of Boccaccio and Dante. It is a dream-allegory, relating how the birds meet on St Valentine's day to choose their mates and how the eagles, who represent the royal lovers, receive the precedence. The chief fascination of the poem lies in the delicacy of its courtly compliment and its naïve and quiet humour. *Troilus and Criseyde* probably dates from 1382 or later. It is a very long poem, and the *Canterbury Tales* apart, Chaucer's most ambitious effort. It is founded on the *Filostrato* of Boccaccio, though the story was already well known before it reached his hands, was, in fact, one of the world's great love-tales.

Chaucer takes the Italian poem mainly as a theme upon which to embroider and invents about two-thirds of the total result. He has very greatly changed the characters, making both hero and heroine more attractive, and he has re-created the character of Pandarus. The scene is laid in the Homeric age but, without the slightest consciousness of anachronism, Chaucer has employed throughout the manners and customs of the Middle Ages. The poem has its faults—it contains far too many digressions —but it embodies the very heart and soul of romance and its psychology of love is subtle and true. The general atmosphere of passion reminds the reader of *Romeo and Juliet* and, in Pandarus, Chaucer has given one of the great comic creations of English literature; Pandarus is guilty of one particularly gross fault and many minor ones; but his geniality and humour leave an unfailing impression upon the mind. The work is full of the richest poetry.

The *Hous of Fame* is usually dated about 1384. It returns to the octosyllabic couplet and the dream-allegory; it seems to have been composed either hastily or somewhat carelessly, for it is not well conceived as a whole and was left unfinished. The allegory is very difficult to interpret and we may doubt if it has been fully understood. The main substance is a reflection on earthly fame, its transitory nature, its uncertainty, the injustice with which it is awarded. The many reminiscences of Dante and the long epitome of the *Aeneid* which occurs early in the poem seem to suggest that Chaucer had been meditating on the glory of the poetic craft as exemplified in Virgil and Dante the great disciple of Virgil, perhaps desirous to emulate both; but had been distracted by the temptation to involve himself in worldly affairs (such perhaps as his plunge into politics with the Parliament of 1386) in which he would gain no honour or, at any rate, only an imperfect and uncertain honour, very unlike the enduring glory of the great poets. Since John of Gaunt was lord of the 'manor of Eagle' the eagle's drastic interference with the poet and his snatching him away from the contemplation of Virgil would be easily explicable. However this may be, the poem contains many admirable examples of that 'elvish' humour which was so marked a feature of Chaucer's character.

The *Legend of Good Women* (usually dated 1386) is the first of Chaucer's poems composed in the ten-syllabled or heroic couplet; this had for some time been one of the favourite metres for French poetry and Chaucer, by his masterly employment of it, made it one of the standard metres for English.

The *Legend*, as has been said, is plainly intended as a compliment to the queen in return for some service. In the prologue Anne of Bohemia, in the allegorical disguise of Alcestis, defends the poet against the attacks of Cupid, and the poet promises to make amends for his slanders upon women by narrating the lives of women who have been martyrs to love or as he says elsewhere the 'Seintes Legends of Cupyde.' Chaucer gives a fascinating portrait of the queen.

The heroines treated of in the *Legend* are all classical, selected largely from Ovid. They are rather curiously chosen, for some of them, such as Cleopatra and Medea, can hardly be regarded as 'seintes' in any sense of the term. Nine stories are told, brief but fine examples of narrative, and then the poem breaks off. Chaucer probably found that the plan was too monotonous and that the stories, with their predestined tragic endings, were becoming, in the mass, too sombre.

He laid it aside for a work which permitted of more variety and provided full scope for his humour.

The *Canterbury Tales* are Chaucer's greatest achievement because they embody his most mature and varied work. In them he reveals himself emphatically as the greatest narrative poet of the English language and, indeed, one of the great narrative poets of the world. He has gained the perfect knowledge of all that makes a good story—not too long, continually reminding both himself and the reader that prolixity destroys interest; on the other hand he is not too brief; he allows himself sufficient room for humorous dialogue, sufficient space to develop character and at times, as in the *Knight's Tale*, for really gorgeous description. The tales themselves are excellent, but the links between are better still; these links are really a continuation of the general Prologue; they show the best comic dialogue which we possess before the time of Shakespeare and suggest that, in a different age, Chaucer might have been a dramatist of the rarest kind.

His power of character-drawing is revealed at its best in his masterpiece—the general Prologue.

Chaucer's method is the ordinary mediaeval method, that is, he does not describe individuals as such but types; the conception of the individual as interesting in himself, independently of his profession or his rank, hardly seems to have occurred to the mediaeval mind; on the other hand, they take the keenest pleasure in showing the impress of a man's trade and profession in moulding his nature and Chaucer is a master of this craft.

Thus the Reve rides ever 'the hindreste of our route' and this is characteristic of the man for his whole life consists of spying upon and watching his subordinates; the Knight rides in a doublet of fustian stained with the marks of his armour which reveals at once how well accustomed he is to the life of adventure and travel and how completely it has become a second nature; the 'brown visage' of the Yeoman suggests his open-air life and the sheaf of 'pecok arwes' the merriment of Merrie England. Each detail is intensely significant; the art of selection, in every craft significant of the master, has never been carried to greater perfection than here.

The *Canterbury Tales* are not quite continuous; the links between break at times so that the tales themselves fall into groups which critics designate as A, B, C, etc.

Chaucer is careful to vary the tales within the same groups so that he passes from romantic to humorous, refined to broad, etc.

Among the romantic tales we may include the *Knight's*, the *Squire's*, the *Franklin's*, etc. The *Knight's Tale* leads off and is the most ambitious of the whole series; it is adapted from Boccaccio's epic—the *Teseide*—which Chaucer considerably abbreviates. It is a noble poem, abounding in imagination, exalted in its tone and temper; its defect lies in a certain conventionality of theme and character. Those portions of the poem which linger in the memory are the descriptions which, in their own way, have never been surpassed: the description of the heroine Emily: 'that fairer was to sene than is the lilie

upon his stalke grene,' of the May morning in the forest
when the 'bisy larke' begins to sing and

> ' Al the Orient laugheth of the light,'

the description of the three temples, the two gorgeous
portraits of Lygurge the king of Thrace and Emetreus
the king of Inde, portraits that glow with manly beauty
and manly power and breathe the very soul of chivalry.

There can hardly be much doubt that a considerable
portion of the *Knight's Tale* is planned in honour of
John of Gaunt; the great tournament arranged by
Theseus is the climax of the *Knight's Tale*, everything
in the action works up to that, and we know that John
of Gaunt was the chief European patron of tournaments;
those he held were international like the one in the
Knight's Tale and champions came from all parts of
Europe. We might also observe that there was a specially
magnificent tournament held in England in 1390 which
was proclaimed in Scotland, Hainault, Germany, Flanders and France; they were, indeed, the great aristocratic sport.

Again, Theseus constructs magnificent temples with
gorgeously decorated walls and architecture was also a
passion with John of Gaunt whose palace of the Savoy
was famous as the most magnificent palace in England
and one of the finest in Europe.

Again, Theseus conducts a war against Thebes and
takes prisoner two young princes, one of whom escapes.
So John of Gaunt had kept in his palace—John—the
captive king of France; John's place was afterwards
taken by his young sons and one of these, weary of what
seemed an interminable imprisonment, broke his parole
and escaped. Theseus has also a great love of hunting
and this again was a favourite taste with John of Gaunt.

The *Squire's Tale* is a story of Eastern magic; it ends
abruptly but, even as it stands, it is one of the most
fascinating of Chaucer's works and would, if completed,
have been a fitting pendant to the *Knight's Tale*; here,
centuries before Coleridge, Chaucer has anticipated his

secret of making the supernatural seem plausible by the truth of the feelings and sensations with which it is associated. The poem has been estimated, whether rightly or not, to have been intended ultimately as a piece of court-compliment[1]. Its material is certainly part of that 'matter of the east' which we owe to the Crusades, and its composition may well have been suggested by the visit of Henry of Derby to the Holy Land.

The saint legends include a good deal of early and rather inferior work, such as in the *Second Nun's Tale* and the *Man of Law's Tale*. The so-called 'Fabliaux' provide us with an absolutely different type. They are tales of contemporary life, dealing with the lower middle-class—millers, carpenters, etc.—and are related with the utmost possible realism. They are all coarse, suggesting Boccaccio or even, at times, Rabelais; but the humour is splendid and every detail vivid; the general atmosphere is what the narrators themselves would call 'jolly' and they give us the most vivid picture we possess of the England of that day with its quaint peculiarities of dress and custom; a masterly portrait, for example, is that of 'Absolon' the parish clerk, whose yellow hair is elaborately curled, and stands out 'as broad as a fan,' parted with exact and precise neatness down the middle; he has the most ornate shoes and red stockings; his 'kirtel' is of light blue and he wears a surplice as white as 'the flower of the rye.' Absolon is accomplished in dancing country dances, 'casting his legs to and fro,' in singing and playing on a small 'rubible' (*i.e.* fiddle). Also he thinks himself irresistible. From the purely literary point of view Chaucer's 'Fabliaux' are among his best works though their coarseness has prevented them from being generally known. Of the fable proper there are three examples, two of the beast fable—the *Nonnë Prestes Tale* and the *Manciple's*—and one moral fable—the *Pardoner's Tale*. The latter is the most grimly impressive thing which Chaucer ever penned. The scene is laid in 'Flanders' in a time of pestilence which is described briefly; but with the sombre

[1] Brandl.

realism of one who had seen it with his own eyes; three 'rioters,' beside themselves with recklessness and arrogance, insolently determine to go in search of the rascal 'Death' who is slaying so many; they are directed to him by an old man who tells them they will find him under a certain tree; they discover there a great heap of gold which does indeed, by their mutual treachery and murder, bring about the destruction of all three. The sombre power of the narrative is in startling contrast to the cynical humour of the Pardoner's own prologue.

A curious group is formed by the mediaeval prose sermons of which there are two specimens—the *Tale of Melibeus* (told by Chaucer himself) and the *Persoun's Tale*; these are good examples of 14th century prose but there is nothing either original or interesting in their subjects.

Every reader of Chaucer must be impressed by the combination in him of what might seem the most opposite qualities: on the one side he is abstract, ideal and chivalrous, beautiful as Spenser himself; on the other side he is as absolutely true to life and as coarsely realistic as Fielding.

He draws with equal zest the portraits of Emetreus of Inde and of Absolon the parish clerk, the one the very soul of chivalry and the other the consummation of amusing absurdity.

One cannot help suspecting that the real point of the contrast lies in Chaucer's desire to please his aristocratic patrons or possibly in his natural tendency to acquiesce in their ideas. At any rate he never applies his mordant humour to the dissection of that aristocratic world itself which must surely, had he treated it realistically, have provided him with almost as many subjects as the Church and the middle classes. The character of Pandarus is the only exception to this rule, and its startling success shows us what he could have done had he so desired.

II

CHRONOLOGICAL TABLES

A

CHAUCER'S LIFE

1340. Birth of Geoffrey Chaucer. This date is uncertain.

1357. In the household accounts of Elizabeth, Duchess of Clarence, mention is made of clothes and other articles purchased for 'Geoffrey Chaucer' who has the standing of a page.

1359. Chaucer joins the military expedition to France and is made prisoner.

1360. Chaucer is ransomed from imprisonment, Edward III contributing towards his ransom £16. The war ends with the treaty of Bretigny.

1366. A pension is granted to a certain 'Philippa Chaucer,' one of the queen's ladies, which pension is afterwards paid through her husband Geoffrey Chaucer.

1367. A pension is granted to Chaucer as one of the valets of the king's household.

1369. Blanche, the first wife of John of Gaunt, dies at the age of twenty-nine; Chaucer writes in her honour the poem entitled *The Dethe of Blaunche the Duchesse* or *The Book of the Duchesse*.

1372. Chaucer, acting with two others, is sent on a mission to Genoa concerning trade. He remained in Italy for six months and probably met Petrarch at Padua.

1374. Chaucer is granted a pitcher of wine daily to be received from the king's butler, a gift afterwards commuted for a yearly pension of 20 marks.

On June 8th he is appointed Controller of the Customs in Wool, Skins and Leather for the port of London.

A few days later he and his wife Philippa receive a pension of £10 a year for life in recompense for services rendered by them.

1377. Chaucer is sent on important missions to Flanders and to France.

In June Edward III dies and is succeeded by his grandson Richard II.

1378. Chaucer, in company with three knights, is sent on a mission to France to negotiate for the marriage of Richard II to 'a daughter of France'; the project comes to nothing.

In the same year he accompanies Sir Edward de Berkeley to Italy on a mission to Bernabo Visconti, tyrant of Milan. He appoints the poet Gower as one of his agents to represent him during his absence.

1381. The pension of Geoffrey Chaucer and his wife Philippa is confirmed by Richard II.

1382. Richard II marries Anne of Bohemia. Chaucer is appointed Controller of the Petty Customs in addition to his former office but is permitted to exercise the functions of the new post by deputy.

1384. He is allowed a deputy for his former office—as Controller of the Wool Quay at London, and is probably indebted to the queen for this favour.

1386. Chaucer is elected Knight of the Shire for Kent. The Parliament of this year compels the king to grant a patent by which he is deprived of power and the supreme authority falls into the hands of Gloucester.

Chaucer loses his two Controllerships and is reduced to raising money on his pensions. In October occurs the Scrope and Grosvenor trial in which Chaucer is described as 'XL ans et plus' and is said to have borne arms for twenty-seven years.

1387. The death of Philippa Chaucer.

1389. Richard II takes the government into his own hands and John of Gaunt returns to England. The Lancastrian party is again in power and Chaucer receives the appointment of Clerk of the King's Works at the Palace of Westminster, the Tower of London, etc.

1390. Chaucer is appointed on a Commission with five others to repair the banks of the Thames between Woolwich and Greenwich.

He is also appointed joint Forester (with Richard Brittle) of North Petherton Park in Somerset.

1391. Chaucer loses his appointment as 'Clerk of the Works.'

1394. Chaucer receives a grant from the king of £20 a year for life.

1395. Chaucer is in pecuniary difficulties and raises money in advance on his pensions.

1398. Chaucer is still in difficulties and the king grants him letters of protection against creditors.

1399. Henry of Lancaster is declared king on Sept. 30th. Chaucer addresses to him a poem entitled 'Compleynt to his Empty Purse' and the king doubles his pension.

1400. Chaucer dies; the date given upon his tombstone is Oct. 25th, 1400.

B

CHAUCER'S WORKS

FIRST PERIOD   —1369

The A B C : a poem so called because each stanza begins with a different letter of the alphabet: it is a hymn to the Virgin paraphrased from a French poet—Guillaume de Deguilevile.

The Compleynt to Pite : a brief and artificial love-poem.

The Romaunt of the Rose : a translation from the French *Roman de la Rose* by the two poets Guillaume de Lorris and Jean de Meung. The first part is a love-allegory, the second resolves itself into a satire upon women and upon the clergy.

The Dethe of Blaunche the Duchesse or the *Book of the Duchesse :* a poem suggested by the death of Blanche of Lancaster, dated 1369 by its subject. A portion of this (ll. 62–222) probably represents an earlier poem—the *Ceys and Alcione* mentioned in the head-link to the *Man of Law's Tale.*

The Lyf of Saint Cecyle : probably but not certainly of this period. Afterwards made the *Second Nun's Tale.*

The Monk's Tale : a series of tragedies dealing with the lives of great men, beginning with Lucifer and Adam and coming down to Chaucer's own contemporaries. Four of these lives were probably added later as that of Bernabo Visconti cannot possibly be early.

Lyrical Poems. Chaucer says that he wrote a large number of 'balades, roundels, virelayes' most of which appear to have been lost.

SECOND PERIOD 1369—1386

The Man of Law's Tale: a saint-legend based upon the Anglo-Norman Chronicle of Nicholas Trivet.

The Clerk's Tale: this cannot be earlier than 1373 as it is founded on Petrarch's Latin version of the story of Griseldis which was made in that year.

Palamon and Arcite: a poem either identical with the *Knight's Tale* or on the same subject, possibly in seven-lined stanza.

Compleynte to his Lady: a brief love-poem.

Anelida and Arcite: a short incomplete love-poem, containing several stanzas translated from the *Teseide.*

The Tale of Melibeus: partly translated from Albertano of Brescia and included in the *Canterbury Tales* as the second one chosen by Chaucer.

The Parlement of Foules: an allegorical poem to celebrate a royal betrothal, probably that of Richard II to Anne of Bohemia: dated 1382 by its subject.

The Persoun's Tale: a mediaeval sermon.

Troilus and Criseyde: adapted from Boccaccio's *Filostrato* with a few stanzas from the *Teseide.* Dated 1382 or later by a reference to Anne of Bohemia.

Boëthius: a translation of the 'De Consolatione Philosophiae'; its author Boëthius, the most learned philosopher of his time, was born at Rome about A.D. 480 and put to death by the emperor Theodoric the Goth in A.D. 524.

There are so many references to this work in *Troilus and Criseyde* that Chaucer was probably intent upon both about the same time.

The Hous of Fame: probably written about 1383 or 4; it seems to be a lament by Chaucer over the burdensome nature of his duties.

LAST PERIOD 1386—1400

The Legend of Good Women. This must be dated later than the preceding works since it mentions the most important among them. It is dedicated to the queen in an allegorical prologue and breaks off after nine tales.

The Canterbury Tales. These do not form one continuous group, for the links connecting them fail in places. From the references to time it is evident that they are supposed to be told on four different days. The total work is only about a quarter of the original plan: Chaucer had intended that each pilgrim should tell four tales, two on the outward journey and two on the homeward (Prologue 791–5), but in the actual form no pilgrim tells more than one except Chaucer himself and he only because his first tale—*Sir Thopas*—is interrupted by the host. No member of the group of mechanics tells a tale nor does the Yeoman, though the tale of Gamelyn, which is the same story as that of *As You Like It*, is included in some mss. as his; it would have been a very suitable subject for the Yeoman and probably represents rough material which Chaucer intended to work up. Two unexpected pilgrims—a Canon and his Yeoman—join on the route, and the Yeoman tells a tale which exposes his master's practices in alchemy.

C

ORDER OF THE CANTERBURY TALES

GROUP A.

General Prologue. Knight's Tale. Miller's Tale. Reeve's Tale. Cook's Tale.

GROUP B.

Man of Law's Tale. Shipman's Tale. Prioress's Tale. Tale of Sir Thopas (Chaucer). *Tale of Melibeus* (Chaucer). *Monk's Tale. Nonnë Prestes Tale.*

GROUP C.

Physician's Tale. Pardoner's Tale.

GROUP D.

Wyf of Bath's Tale. Friar's Tale. Summoner's Tale.

GROUP E.

Clerk's Tale. Merchant's Tale.

GROUP F.

Squire's Tale. Franklin's Tale.

GROUP G.

Second Nun's Tale. Canon's Yeoman's Tale.

GROUP H.

Manciple's Tale.

GROUP I.

Persoun's Tale.

According to the notes of place and time mentioned on the way Group A seems to have been intended for relation on the first day, Group B on the second day, Groups C, D and E on the third day and the remainder on the fourth.

III

INTRODUCTION TO THE 'PRIORESS'S TALE'

CHAUCER'S *Prioress's Tale* is exquisitely suited to the character of the narrator; its stanza form suggests that it may be comparatively early work; but its perfection and delicacy show us a talent fully matured and so probably later than the *Clerk's Tale* or the *Man of Law's*; it may have been written for direct insertion in the *Canterbury Tales*.

In the year 1386, as has been said, Philippa Chaucer together with Henry, Earl of Derby (afterwards Henry IV), Sir Thomas de Swynford and six others were admitted into the fraternity of Lincoln Cathedral, John of Gaunt being present at the ceremony. Hugh of Lincoln, whose story, as Chaucer himself points out, so closely resembles that of the *Prioress's Tale*:

> 'O yonge Hugh of Lincoln, slayn also
> With cursed Jewes as it is notable,'

was one of the canonised saints of the cathedral and his tomb was shown to visitors in Chaucer's day and for centuries later. A coffin was opened in the year 1791 beneath a shrine traditionally associated with St Hugh and was found to contain the remains of a boy about the eight years of age ascribed to the martyr.

So also in Chaucer's time and for many centuries later visitors to Lincoln were shown the well adjoining the Jews' Court into which the body of Hugh had been thrown. It is surely exceedingly probable that Chaucer may have been present at the ceremony and that he should have become interested in the local legend and inspired to write one closely resembling it. If this suggestion be plausible we are, however, at once prompted to enquire why Chaucer did not himself tell the tale of Hugh of Lincoln instead of one differing in several important points and possessing only a general similarity. The probable answer is that the original tale of little Sir Hugh would be a subject too gruesome for the tender-hearted Prioress. According to the story as given by Matthew Paris and other chroniclers the child was imprisoned by the Jews and executed in mockery of the crucifixion; for three days he was exposed to the most exquisite tortures; he was scourged, he was crowned with thorns, he was pierced with a knife and made to drink gall, etc. Every detail of the sufferings of Christ was wreaked upon his little body. Such a hideous martyrdom for a mere child would surely have been too dreadful a subject for the Prioress; in fact we may note that Chaucer does not like horrible subjects and very rarely selects any; he takes the tale of Ugo from Dante but even that he softens by dwelling mainly on its pathos, not its horror; Chaucer, in fact, had a tenderness which made him dislike the last extremity of human suffering and he almost always declines to face it, in this differing both from Dante and from Shakespeare.

So in the *Prioress's Tale* he passes by the awful legend of Hugh of Lincoln and chooses one resembling it but capable of being made much sweeter and gentler. Chaucer's 'little clergeon' meets his fate swiftly and mercifully; there is no imprisonment, there are no long tortures, there is no ghastly mockery of Christ; he is killed but without torment.

Another element of pity, particularly appropriate to the Prioress, is introduced by connecting the tale with the figure of the Virgin; she adds a note of maternal tenderness and beauty; the 'little clergeon' is not left alone in his awful ordeal; a compassionate figure watches over him, comforts him and will not forsake him until his body is found and laid in sacred earth. Indeed, if the parallel tales are closely examined, it will be seen how careful Chaucer is to dwell on the fact, which none of the other versions make so clear, that the child never really suffers the last extremity of pain for he is always consoled.

Both tales—Hugh of Lincoln's and the Prioress's—belong to that large collection of mediaeval legends concerned with the blood accusation against the Jews. In Chaucer's England the Jews were unknown, at least under their own name. In early mediaeval England the Jewish race had played a prominent part. Chaucer represents them in his tale as being under the especial protection of the 'lord of that country' who supported them because of their usury:

> 'Sustened by a lord of that contree
> For foule usure and lucre of vilanye.'

This was exactly the position the English Jews had held in the early Middle Ages as is made plain by the laws of Edward the Confessor: 'Be it known that all Jews, wheresoever they may be in the realm, are of right under the tutelage and protection of the King; nor is it lawful for any of them to subject himself to any wealthy person without the King's license; for the Jews and all their effects are the King's property; and if anyone withhold their money from them let the King recover it as his own.'

The Jews were, as the above plainly shows, treated as a direct perquisite of the Crown.

William the Conqueror made similar regulations and especially invited the Jews from Rouen in Normandy to settle in England.

The Jews were the great capitalists of the Middle Ages, for the Canon Law forbade Christians to lend out money at interest; thus the Jews for a long period had a monopoly of all capitalist transactions and the king obtained a very considerable revenue from them in exchange for licenses to trade and so forth. The system may be best summarised by saying that the Jews were permitted to fleece thoroughly the people of the realm on condition that the king fleeced them. This is the main cause of the extraordinary hatred of Jews shown throughout mediaeval Europe; they were the great extortioners and usurers and they were also the agents of royal tyranny and oppression. In England this cause for animosity was greatly increased by political events. The Commons continually struggled to obtain a measure of popular control over the throne and their great weapon was the power of the purse; but the king, by appealing to the Jews, could evade the people's chief weapon by making himself independent of their supplies. Thus Parliament was forced to the conclusion that political liberty was impossible without the expulsion of the Jews. In the reign of Edward I the Commons prevailed upon the king to pass an act against usury (1278) which took away the official standing of the Jews and further persuaded him to expel them (in 1290); the Commons taxed themselves very heavily in order to get rid of the Jews, and there is no doubt that their expulsion was a thoroughly popular measure; over sixteen thousand left the country. Their place as capitalists was taken by the Italian bankers, the Bardi and the Perussi and others. The Jews were not allowed to return to England openly until the time of Cromwell; but there must have been a good many who returned disguised as foreigners of various nationalities.

The Crusades, by the religious feelings they excited, increased the animosity against Jews and, in various parts of Europe, there arose the dreadful blood accusation: the accusation that the Jewish race kidnapped children for ritual murder.

Hyamson[1] says: 'The eloquence and zeal of Peter the Hermit and his coadjutors in the preaching of the First Crusade succeeded in banding together men of all nations in the task of recovering the Holy Land....They had, however, another result that was hardly intended. To rouse the passions of the soldiers of the Cross lurid tales were told of all that Christians had suffered at the hands of that eastern people estranged from God and the enemies of Christ....Men and women had been tortured, Christians circumcised and their blood used for superstitious purposes....The Jews were regarded as the allies of these torturers. The Crusaders in their march left behind them a trail of martyred Jews. Community after community from France to Hungary was utterly destroyed.'

It is easy to understand how Chaucer, if he stood at the tomb of Hugh of Lincoln with a Crusader (Henry of Derby) at his side, could associate his tale of ritual murder with the land to which the knight intended to journey and actually did journey (1390).

It is almost certainly the association of ritual murder with the Crusades that makes him lay the scene of his tale in Asia:

> 'There was in Asie, in a greet citee
> Amonges Cristen folk, a Jewerye.'

In England the blood accusation was repeatedly brought against the Jews. There were numerous such cases: in 1168 against the Jews of Gloucester, in 1181 at Bury St Edmunds, in London in 1244. In every case a shrine and miracles attached themselves to the burial-

---

[1] *History of the Jews in England.*

place of the victim which, of course, was usually in the local
abbey or cathedral. Chaucer is thus historically accurate
when he represents his murdered boy as taken to the
'nexte abbey' and buried with great honour by the whole
convent, the abbot in person conducting the service and
the population in deep mourning; he is equally accurate in
speaking of the beautiful tomb 'of marbul-stones clere.'

The hostility between the townsfolk and the Jews is
again true to historic fact. Hyamson says: 'When the
Jews were in need of protection against the violence of
the townsfolk, it was in the Royal Castle that they, as a
rule, took refuge and the king's sheriff with his following
who came to their defence.'

Yet again Chaucer has historical warrant in representing the Jews as exasperated by the hymn to the Virgin,
for they frequently showed extreme resentment at
Christian usages and observances.

To quote Hyamson: 'The votaries of mediaeval
Christianity were also exasperated by the critical in-
credulity with which the Jews received the pretended
miracles and the adoration of images....The Jews were
not satisfied to cast ridicule in private among themselves
upon manifestations; in several instances they interrupted religious observances with their criticisms greatly
to the indignation of the participators and also to the
inconvenience and punishment of the critics.'

So Chaucer represents their bitter anger at the hymn
'Alma Redemptoris Mater':

> 'Is this to you a thing that is honest?'

they enquire of each other.

Another accurate detail is the method of punishment
inflicted; thus Matthew Paris records that, in the case of
Hugh of Lincoln, the Jew—Copin—was tied to a horse's
tail and dragged to the gallows. It was, in fact, the usual
method of execution in such cases.

Chaucer has:

> 'Therfor with wilde hors he dide hem drawe,
> And after that he heng hem by the lawe.'

There are in English a number of popular ballads on the subject of a Christian boy murdered by Jews; most of them resemble Chaucer's tale far more closely than they resemble the story of Hugh as given by Matthew Paris.

The general outline of all these ballads is the same. A boy is playing near the Jewish quarter; the Jew's daughter entices him to enter her father's house, usually with the lure of an apple; when she gets him alone she murders him, sticking him with a knife 'like a swine' and his body is cast in a deep draw-well. The body, however, by a miracle, continues to speak and is heard either by the mother or some schoolmate. The crime is thus revealed and the Jews are punished. The popular ballad in Percy's version (published 1765) places the scene in Mirry-land town (Merry Lincoln) and gives a dialogue between the boy and his mother; as in Chaucer's version the boy speaks to her from a well. In Jamieson's version the Virgin is insulted because the body of the boy is thrown into 'our Lady's well' and hence makes the matter her own concern.

In Motherwell's version a schoolboy, walking in a garden, hears moaning in a well and summons help and in Hume's version the child sends affecting messages to his playfellow.

All these popular English variants are, of course, as we have them, later than Chaucer's day; neither do they appear to have been derived from the same original as his story, for in most the figure of the Virgin plays no part and in none has she anything like the prominence assigned by Chaucer; the probability is that the folk ballads are all more or less popularised versions of Hugh of Lincoln.

The closest analogues to Chaucer's story, and therefore those most likely to be his sources, are to be found in mediaeval French; these may be themselves suggested by the tale of Hugh; but they take a different turn, connecting the whole story with the Virgin and making it one of her miracles.

The first of these tales is by Gautier de Coincy (1177–1266) and is included in his *Miracles de la Sainte Vierge*. The author narrates that he has been greatly rejoiced by a miracle which occurred formerly in England: there was a poor widow who loved very greatly the sweet lady 'la douce dame'; she had to work very hard for her living; she had one son and no more; but he was a very beautiful boy whom she dearly loved and she sent him quite young to school; the Virgin caused him to learn well and fast so that he could achieve more in one half-year than others could in four and he soon knew how to sing and how to read:

> 'le mere deu, qui entremete
> Se vost d'aidier le clerconcel
> dedanz son cuer e i moncel
> Amoncela si grant savoir,
> L'an demi an li fist savoir
> Plus c'un autre ne set en quatre
>
> .   .   .   .
> Tost sot chanter et tost sot lire.'

The child took great pains; all who heard him praised his voice and his skill and he soon earned enough to support himself and his mother. One of his songs was the 'Gaude Maria'; it is, says the narrative, a sweet and pitiful, a delightful and beautiful song:

> 'Entre ses biaus chans qu'il savoit
> le biau respons apris avoit
> de la purificacion
> Qui gaude maria a non;
> le diz en est douz et piteus
> et li chans biauz et deliteus.'

One day he was playing with his friends in the Jewish quarter when a crowd collected who asked him to sing the 'Gaude Maria':

> 'Tuit li prient que sanz delai
> de nostre dame i petit chant.'

He sang so well that even the 'felon Jews' came to hear:

> 'Nes le juif, li felon chien,
> I sont venus avec les autres.'

When the Jews heard the 'Gaude Maria' one among
them was so greatly enraged that he wished to kill the
boy but dared not act immediately; he waited till the
crowd had dispersed and then enticed the child into his
house, promising him a reward if he sang his beautiful
song. The child entered and the Jew, having him alone,
killed him with an axe, made a grave under the door and
buried him. The child's mother went weeping through
the town enquiring his whereabouts from everyone she
met; she spent the night weeping and imploring the
Virgin to aid her; the next day she was informed that
her child had been seen in the Jews' quarter and that it
was probable they had killed him. Three weeks elapsed
before the sorrowing mother received news of her son;
then the Virgin caused the child, dead and buried though
it was, to sing the 'Gaude Maria' in a loud voice; the
crowd forced their way into the Jew's house and, guided
by the song, dug up the body; they found the child safe
and sound for the Virgin had miraculously healed him;
he told the tale of his death and burial and of how the
Virgin appeared to him and commanded him to sing:

> 'la douce mere debonaire
> Atant ne departi de moi,
> et ie au plus haut que ie poi,
> Encomencai le bel respons.'

The people rang the bells with joy at this great miracle
and several Jews became converted to Christianity. The
moral of the whole tale is, of course, that the man does
well who serves the Virgin both day and night.

It can be seen that this tale presents several very
interesting parallels to that of Chaucer; it is a miracle of
the Virgin and the boy hero is a chorister by profession
who brings his fate upon himself by his devotion to the
Virgin and the hymns he sings in her honour. On the
other hand, Chaucer's miracle is far less gross and ex-
travagant.

Another parallel, even closer, is to be found in the tale
of the Paris beggar-boy murdered by a Jew for singing
'Alma Redemptoris Mater'; this is, of course, the exact

song of Chaucer's chorister. The tale is found in a collection entitled *The Miracles of the Virgin* in the Vernon
MS. in the Bodleian dated about 1375 A.D.

It narrates how there was a poor beggar-boy in Paris
who earned a livelihood for himself and his parents by
singing:

> 'The child non othar . Craftes couthe
> But winne his lyflode . with his Mouthe!
> the Childes vois . was swete and cler
> Men lusted his song . with riht good cher.
>
> .   •   .   •   .   •   .   •   .
>
> Hit was an Antimne . of ure lady,
> He song that Antimne . everi wher,
> I-called . Alma Redemptoris Mater,
> that is forthrihtly . to mene:
> Godus Moder . Mylde and Clene,
> Hevene yate . and sterre of se,
> Save thi peple . from synne and we.'

He sang this song once on Saturday through the Jewry
and a Jew enticed the boy into his house and cut his
throat: the child, however, continues to sing and the Jew
in terror throws his body into a privy:

> 'the child a-down ther . Inne he throng.
> The child song evere . the same song,
> So lustily . the child con crie
> that song he never er . so hyge,
> Men mihte him here . fer and neer;
> The Childes vois was . so heig and cleer!'

His mother seeks for him and hears his voice in the
Jewry; she follows its guidance; the Jew denies that the
boy is there but the child continues to sing. The mother
goes in search of the Mayor and bailiffs and makes a
complaint, the Mayor gathers the people of the town and
they all visit the Jewry and hear the voice:

> 'Anon they herde . the childes voyse,
> Riht as an Angels vois . hit were,
> thei herde him never . synge so clere.'

The people sought until they found the child's body in
the privy covered with filth and were filled with amaze-
ment; the Bishop came to search into the miracle and

to discover what it was that made the child continue to sing:

> 'the child song evere . iliche clere.
> the Bisschop serchede . with his hond:
> withinne the childes . throte he fond
> A lilie flour . so briht and cler
> So feir a lylie . nas nevere seyn er,
> with guildene lettres . everi wher:
> Alma Redemptoris . Mater
> Anon that lilie . out was taken,
> the childes song . bigon to slaken
> that swete song . was herd no more
> But as a ded cors the child lay there.'

The Bishop commands that the body shall be borne in state through the city; it is accompanied by priests and clerks with chanting and ringing of the bells. In the Minster they commence the mass of Requiem; but the body rises and begins to sing the 'Salve sancta parens.'

It was thus easy for men to know the truth, namely that the child had always honoured the sweet lady. Here, as we see at once, the parallel to Chaucer is even closer. We have the exact hymn to the Virgin sung by Chaucer's chorister; we have also the conception of the Virgin laying a charm upon his tongue to give him the power to sing: but here again Chaucer has mitigated the supernatural; the lily flower laid on the child's tongue seems too clumsy and the miracle by which he rises after death and sings is, once more, too gross. It is not until we compare Chaucer in detail with those tales which most closely resemble his that we fully realise the exquisite fineness of his art.

We may also observe a few facts regarding mediaeval schools. Chaucer's 'little clergeon' was a chorister and there were special schools for such children.

Mediaeval schools were of different types: the most elementary were the A, B, C schools and in these the instruction was very simple and only suitable for very young children. Song schools were on a higher level: their chief object was to train choristers in music and singing in order that they might be able to assist the priests in the services of the church; as a rule they taught also reading and writing; writing was, however, considered less important than reading or singing and much less time was spent upon it.

'Grammar' meant Latin Grammar and was taught in the higher grade schools.

Chaucer, of course, is simply transferring the customs of his own England to the nameless town in Syria. The school to which his little chorister goes is plainly a 'song school,' for he studies his 'antiphoner' or anthem book containing words and music and he learns from his primer; his school is not a Grammar school, for he does not know any Latin and even his elder schoolmate knows but little.

Chaucer's Prioress is described in the Prologue in a picture of unforgettable humour and grace:

> 'Ther was also a Nonne, a Prioresse,
> That of hir smylyng was ful symple and coy;
> Hire gretteste ooth was but by seintë Loy,
> And she was cleped madame Eglentyne.
> Ful weel she song the service dyuyne,
> Entuned in hir nose ful semely,
> And Frenssh she spak ful faire and fetisly
> After the scole of Stratford-atte-Bowe,
> For Frenssh of Parys was to hire unknowe.
> At mete wel y-taught was she with alle,
> She leet no morsel from hir lippes falle,
> Ne wette hir fyngres in hir sauce depe.
> Wel koude she carie a morsel and wel kepe,
> That no drope ne fille upon hire breste;
> In curteisie was set ful muchel hir leste.
> Hire over lippe wyped she so clene,
> That in hir coppe ther was no ferthyng sene
> Of grece, whan she dronken hadde hir draughte.
> Ful semely after hir mete she raughte,
> And sikerly she was of greet desport,
> And ful plesaúnt and amyable of port,
> And peyned hire to countrefete cheere
> Of Court, and been estatlich of manere,
> And to ben holden digne of reverence.
> But for to speken of hire conscience,
> She was so charitable and so pitous

She wolde wepe, if that she saugh a mous
Kaught in a trappe, if it were deed or bledde.
Of smale houndes hadde she that she fedde
With rosted flessh, or milk and wastel breed;
But soore wepte she if oon of hem were deed,
Or if men smoot it with a yerde smerte;
And al was conscience and tendre herte.
Ful semyly hir wympul pynched was;
Hire nose tretys, hir eyen greye as glas,
Hir mouth ful smal and ther-to softe and reed,
But sikerly she hadde a fair forheed;
It was almost a spanne brood I trowe,
For, hardily, she was not undergrowe.
Ful fetys was hir cloke, as I was war;
Of smal coral aboute hire arm she bar
A peire of bedes, gauded al with grene,
And ther on heng a brooch of gold ful sheene,
On which ther was first write a crowned A,
And after Amor vincit omnia.'

It would be a mistake to consider Chaucer's description of her table manners as being in any sense ironic, for beautiful table manners were greatly admired in the Middle Ages and books of etiquette paid attention to just such details as those Chaucer describes. Prioresses, as such, had a certain liberty of travelling outside the convent; the rules for the claustration of nuns were at one time very severe; but they had become somewhat relaxed in the 14th century; certain liberties of travel were permitted especially to the higher ranks and a pilgrimage would assuredly be one.

IV

INTRODUCTION TO 'SIR THOPAS'

CHAUCER'S *Sir Thopas* is a burlesque upon the rhymed romances which were very popular in his day; it ridicules these romances alike in its metre, its theme and its general style. The metre is the ordinary ballad metre so often employed in mediaeval English and also in Scottish poetry both in rhymed romances and in folk-ballads; its scheme is an eight-syllabled couplet followed by a line of six syllables twice repeated.

In ordinary ballad metre the rhymes in the second couplet usually differ from those in the first; but Chaucer, who is a master of skilful and ingenious rhyme, has frequently employed in *Sir Thopas* one rhyme four times repeated which adds to the rollicking effect.

The same metre is employed in *Sir Beves of Hamtoun* one of the poems to which Chaucer alludes:

> 'Loedinges, heareth to me tale!
> Is merier than the nightingale,
>   That y shal singe;
> Of a knight ich wile yow roune
> Beves a highte of Hamtoune,
>   Withouten lesinge.'

A variety of the same metre is also employed in *Sir Gowther* which consists of the same scheme twice repeated.

Chaucer was amused by its monotonous jog-trot which seldom reaches the level of real distinction and hence mimics it with gusto; it is hardly necessary to point out that, for narrative purposes, the metre is far inferior to his own favourites: the seven-lined stanza and the heroic couplet.

The Middle Ages also employed this ballad metre in a form which they called 'rime couvée' or 'tailed' metre with an additional very short line, either included in the stanza or placed at the end; Chaucer gives several instances of this and deliberately makes it as comic as possible:

> 'Anon I slee thy stede
>   With mace.'
>   'Thy mawe
>   Shal I percen if I may.'

The whole course of the poem is also at once an imitation and a mockery of the style of the rhymed romances. These often give a long and elaborate description, like a catalogue, of the beauties of the hero and heroine; Chaucer who himself commenced in this way, as in his description of Blanche in the *Book of the Duchesse*, soon learnt a better method and the portraits of Lycurgus and Demetrius in the *Knight's Tale* are noble instances of the art of selection. To Chaucer's mature genius the catalogue method came to appear thoroughly comic and he turns it to ridicule in his list of the 'beauties' of Sir Thopas; his 'rode' is 'lyk scarlet in grayn,' his hair and beard yellow as 'safroun'; the same thing may be said of the jeering and satirical description of the dress of Sir Thopas which is meant as an ironic contrast to the gorgeous beauty of the true knightly attire as we find it described, for instance, in *Sir Gawayne* and in Demetrius and Lycurgus.

The same thing is true of the description of the plants and the birds; Chaucer himself gives a long list of plants and birds in the *Parlement of Foules* and it was, indeed, a common custom in mediaeval literature; yet Chaucer can perceive its comical side.

The love of a knight for an elf-queen is, again, a common motive in mediaeval romance and occurs in many French tales; so, of course, do giants and conflicts with giants.

In fact Chaucer employs in *Sir Thopas* the stock machinery of the romantic tale; we may observe that Spenser, writing at a later date, took all these properties quite seriously and introduces giants and fairies into his greatest poem though it is true that to Spenser these things are simply symbolic.

Chaucer, as M. Légouis justly points out, has no real affection for the mediaeval romances; he does not mention them often and, even when he does, his tone can hardly be called one of reverence:

'No man but Lancelot and he is deed.'

He does not appear, as has already been pointed out, to have known the best of these romances. Chaucer gives us in *Sir Thopas* a list of those which seem to have especially amused him; they include Horn Child, Sir Bevis of Southampton and Sir Guy of Warwick.

It is certainly appropriate that Chaucer should place

this satire upon the rhymed romances in his own mouth
for it really was his mission in life to carry English literature a long stride in advance and to leave the popular
tales behind; he introduced into the conventional mediaeval world of England a new note of reality, freshness
and truth. He is, therefore, justified in satirising the
popular poetry he leaves behind. Also he probably ridicules popular poetry in exactly the same spirit as that
in which he ridicules popular life.

It remains to be asked if Chaucer has any other motive
in *Sir Thopas* beside that of a literary satire. It is exceedingly probable that he has for *Sir Thopas* certainly
appears to be intended as a satire against Philip van
Artevelde. Chaucer would have many good reasons for
such a satire. As we have seen the Lancastrian party to
which he belonged was the party of the feudal reaction;
all over Europe a great social struggle was proceeding
which might be described as a struggle between the old
feudal nobility and the growing power of the Communes.
This was markedly the case in France, Flanders and England. The terrible disasters of Crecy and Poictiers had dis-
credited the French noblesse and power was for a time
transferred to the hands of the Third Estate. The French
Commons found leaders in Étienne Marcel, provost of
the Merchants of Paris and in Charles the Bad of Navarre.

A similar struggle was also proceeding in England between the Parliament on the one hand and on the other
the feudal nobility of whom John of Gaunt was the head.
The chief European storm-centre was, however, in Flanders where the Flemish burghers carried on a prolonged
and bitter conflict against their hereditary counts and
found as leaders the two van Arteveldes—Jacques and his
son Philip. The king of France naturally supported the
count of Flanders who was his feudal dependant and the
struggle resolved itself into a prolonged and bitter civil
war, involving two generations, the count of Flanders
and his son Louis de Maele on one side and Jacques and
Philip van Artevelde on the other.

Meanwhile the citizens of Paris and London regarded

with the utmost sympathy the struggles of Ghent and Bruges against their overlords. As we can perceive easily enough from the pages of Froissart class consciousness in the 14th century was considerably stronger than national consciousness; all over Europe the feudal aristocracy felt themselves as one body contrasted with the lesser world of the middle classes and the Communes. Froissart, for instance, shows an intense appreciation of the courage and valour of the English chivalry; he dwells with delight on tournaments and all kinds of knightly conflicts; but he has no sympathy with the wretched and down-trodden French peasantry who suffered from the exactions and cruelties of both sides and whose homes and lands were incessantly ravaged.

Now the exploits of the burghers of Ghent and Bruges were a serious matter to this feudal nobility for they threatened a wholly new order of society.

Namèche says: 'The triumph of Philip van Artevelde was looked upon as a triumph of the cities against the nobles.'

Juste[1] remarks: 'An extinguishable thirst for liberty then tormented almost the whole of Europe. Paris, Rheims, Chalons, Orléans, Beauvais, Blois were awaiting the success of the Flamands in order to massacre the nobility....The English towns also followed the example of the Flemish towns in Wat Tyler's rebellion....Froissart states plainly that the gentlemen and nobles would have been doomed had not van Artevelde been crushed.'

Froissart naturally does his utmost to ridicule the leaders of the burghers and treats van Artevelde through-out as a comic character and an absurd pretender. Now Chaucer had exactly the same reasons for satirising van Artevelde as Froissart and also, in addition, other reasons of his own, since Chaucer's patron—John of Gaunt—found his interests in the sharpest possible conflict with those of the Flemish burghers. Through his second wife —Constance of Castile—John of Gaunt laid claim to the

[1] *Histoire de Belgique.*

throne of Castile and he had long pleaded for English support in enforcing this claim. He had obtained Richard's promise for an army and it was precisely at this moment that the Flemish conflict entered into serious rivalry with his own.

It was in the year 1381 that Philip van Artevelde was entreated by the burghers of Ghent to place himself at their head. The Count of Flanders, Louis de Maele, was supported by Charles VI, the young king of France and by the Duke of Burgundy. The burghers, however, notwithstanding the enormous odds, were at first successful and took possession of Bruges while the count fled to France.

The danger of allowing the Flemish revolt to go unpunished was forcibly brought home to the French nobility by rumours of communal conspiracies in their own cities of Paris, Orléans, Rheims, etc. Accordingly elaborate preparations were made to crush the Flamands and, six months after van Artevelde's victory, a numerous French army was prepared under the leadership of Charles VI.

The Gantois appealed to England and the citizens of London and other large towns were anxious to assist; indeed the whole mercantile interest in the Commons was in favour of giving aid to Flanders. Moreover, all the enemies of John of Gaunt, and they were many, proved advocates of the Flemish scheme because it was a rival to his ambition. The Commons would do nothing whatever on the side of Spain. An effort was also made to represent the matter as a religious war and the blessing of the Pope was obtained since he ardently desired to suppress the French schismatics who supported his rival at Avignon, the Avignon pope being practically a vassal of France.

We are now in a position to compare events in Flanders with those of Chaucer's *Sir Thopas*.

In the first place we note that Sir Thopas is a Flemish hero; he is born in

'Flaundres, al biyonde the sea,
    At Poperinghe in the place;
His fader was a man ful free,
    And lord he was of that contree,
       As it was Goddes grace.'

Poperinghe was not the birthplace of Philip van Artevelde; but it was one of the towns which were most zeal-
ous in the league which supported him. Jacques van
Artevelde had devoted himself in a quite special way to
the interests of Poperinghe; there was a league among
the larger towns—Ghent, Bruges—to limit the right of
cloth-making to themselves and to forbid it to the smaller
ones; this would have ruined the smaller towns and they,
Poperinghe prominent among them, resisted bitterly.
Jacques van Artevelde took the part of Poperinghe and
it was the disturbances which resulted that culminated
in his death[1]. Thus Chaucer would have a good deal of
warrant in representing his hero's father as specially connected with Poperinghe. His father is 'lord of that coun-
tree' and we remember that Jacques van Artevelde had
been raised to just such a position of supremacy.

Froissart also has a passage (anno 1382) dealing with
the homage of Poperinghe to Philip van Artevelde:

'la vinrent ceux des châtelleries de outre Ypres, de Fuenes et
de Poperinghen qui se mirent en son obéissance et jurèrent foi
et loyauté à tenir ainsi comme à leur seigneur le comte de
Flandre.'

Sir Thopas is represented throughout in a burlesque
and comic light and that, as has been said, is exactly the
way in which Froissart treats Philip van Artevelde; thus
he represents the kings of France and England as bursting
into laughter when they receive his letters or his em-
bassies:

'Philippe d'Artevelde écrivit unes lettres moult douces et
moult amiables devers le roi de France et son conseil....Le
roi les prit et les fit lire, présents son oncle et son conseil.
Quand on les eut lues et entendues, on n'en fit que rire; et fut

[1] Namèche, *Les van Artevelde*.

adoncques ordonné de retenir le messager et le mettre en prison....Quand Philippe d'Artevelde le sçut, car son messager ne revenoit point, il le prit en grand indignation.'

Froissart also recounts that Philip sent ambassadors to London to ask for help and to request that large sums of money lent some time previously by Flanders should be repaid—a request far from tactful considering the time at which it was made:

'Quand les seigneurs eurent oui cette parole et requête, il commèncerent à regarder l'un l'autre et les aucuns à sourire.'

The ambassadors from Ghent are shown out and, when they are gone, all the council laugh.

Chaucer represents his Sir Thopas as a person attired in an extraordinary fashion which is neither that of a knight nor of a burgher nor any other accepted method of dress. He wears the long beard which was characteristic of the burgher; but certainly not of the helmeted knight:

'his berd was lyk saffroun.
That to his girdel raughte adoun.'

His shoes are of Cordewane (*i.e.* Cordova leather), his hose come from Bruges, his robe is of ciclatoun and, when he is armed, his armour is just as extraordinary, his helmet being of 'laton bright,' his saddle of 'rewel-boon' (*i.e.* whalebone or walrus-ivory) and his warhorse was an 'ambler.'

Now here again we have a parallel with Froissart who represents the Flemish burghers as being attired and armed in the most extraordinary variety of manners. Sir Thopas also is fond of toothsome delicacies; his attendants bring him sweet wine, mead, spices, gingerbread which is especially good, liquorice, cummin seed and sugar. This is thoroughly comic as an account of a knightly banquet; but it does suggest what Froissart says of the delicacies brought to the army of the Flemish burghers:

'Les Flamands avoient en leur ost (before the siege of Audenarde) halles de drap, de pelleteries, de mercerie, et

marché tous les samedis; et leur apportoit on des villages environ toutes choses de douceurs, fruits, beurre, lait, fromages,
poulailles et autres chose...et vins de Rhin, de Poitou, de
France, Malvoisie et autres vins étrangers.'

With regard to the mead—again a curious drink for a
knight—we may observe that the enemies of the van
Arteveldes taunted them with being by trade brewers of
metheglin, *i.e.* beer mixed with honey.

Chaucer's Sir Thopas is a person who loves pastoral
meditations among the birds and flowers; he rejoices to
be in the woods, hearing the songs of the throstle and the
wood-dove. So Froissart represents Philip van Artevelde as having been accustomed, before he was called
to supreme power, to a life of retirement and to have
been very fond of meditation in the fields and of gentle
and solitary occupations such as fishing. It was, says
Froissart, vast presumption in such a recluse to match
himself in wars and battles against great captains:

'Philippe d'Artevelde, quoiqu'il lui fut bien avenu en son
commencement de la Bataille de Bruges, qu'il eût eu cette
grâce et en cette fortune de déconfire le comte et ceux de Bruges,
n'étoit bien subtil à faire guerre ni siéges, car de sa jeunesse il
n'y avoit été point nourri, mais de pêcher à la verge (ligne) aux
poissons en la rivière de l'Escaut et du Lys: de cela faire avoit
il été grand coutumier, et bien le montra, lui étant devant
Audenarde. Car oncque ne sçut la ville asservir (assiéger) et
croyoit bien, par grandeur et présomption qui étoit en lui, que
ceux à Audenarde se dussent venir rendre à lui.'

We may compare this with Hutton[1]:

'Philip van Artevelde appears to have led (up to 1381) an
obscure and tranquil life. He was evidently a dreamer and
little fitted to cope with stern realities.'

Chaucer's Sir Thopas has a romantic adventure with
an elf-queen whom he meets, or dreams he meets, in a
wood by night and who sleeps with him in the open field.
Now Froissart also makes great play with a 'damoiselle'
who accompanied Philip van Artevelde in the field and

---

[1] *The van Arteveldes.*

spent the night with him; modern historians seem agreed
that the accusation is really a slander and that the lady
who accompanied van Artevelde was, as a matter of fact,
his wife; but Froissart certainly represents it as a romantic
and amorous adventure:

'Philippe d'Artevelde avoit à amie une damoiselle de Gand,
laquelle en ce voyage étoit venues avecqùes lui, et pendant
que Philippe dormoit sur une coute pointe près le feu de
charbon en son pavillon, cette femme environ minuit, sortit
hors du pavillon.'

Immediately afterwards, Froissart tells us, a great dis-
turbance is heard and his enemies are upon him almost
exactly as Sir Thopas meets with the giant after the
lady.

Again Chaucer's Sir Thopas meets with a great giant,
Sir Olifaunt (Elephant), who threatens to slay his horse,
who casts many stones at him out of a 'fel staf-slinge'
and who has 'three heads.'

Now Philip van Artevelde had to fight against the
French army which was certainly gigantic as compared
with his own burghers; he had three chief opponents—
Charles VI of France, Louis de Maele and the Duke of
Burgundy; artillery with stones cast from huge slings
certainly played a large part in the French equipment
and at one time the French seriously injured the Flamands by slaying their horses.

With regard to the 'fel staf-slinge' we may observe
that this was the exact principle on which the great
artillery of the Middle Ages was constructed; a 'staff-
sling' was a sling in which additional power was gained
by fastening the little part on to the end of a stick. Now
the artillery employed in the Middle Ages—trebuchet,
mangonel, etc.—simply consisted of enlarged staff-slings
casting great stones. We thus observe that, in Chaucer's
story, all the main details agree: the three-headed giant,
the staff-sling and the slaying of the horses.

Again Chaucer's Sir Thopas keeps royal state in his
own home:

> '"Do come" he seyde "My minstrales,
> And gestours for to tellen tales,
> 　　Anon in myn arminge.
> His merie men commanded he
> To make him both game and glee."'

Now the royal state kept by Philip van Artevelde is one of Froissart's main accusations against him and there is nothing of which he speaks with greater irony; the fact that, like a monarch, he keeps minstrels to play at his meals is one Froissart brings up with special anger:

'tant que il fut à Bruges il tint état de prince car tous les jours par ses menestrels il faisoit sonner et corner devant son hôtel à ses dîners et à ses soupers; et se faisoit servir en vaisselle couverte d'argent, ainsi comme si il fut comte de Flandre; et bien pouvoir tenir cet état, car il avoit toute la vaisselle du comte, d'or et d'argent, et tous les joyaux et sommiers qui avoient été trouvés en l'hôtel du comte à Bruges; ni rien on ne avoit sauvé.'

And again:

'Et adonc se départit Philippe d'Artevelde à quatre milles hommes et prit le chemin de Ypres....Toute manière de gens issirent au devant de lui et le recueillirent aussi honorablement comme si ce fut leur seigneur naturel qui vint premièrement à terre et se mirent tous en son obeissance.'

Froissart says again that Philip van Artevelde 'renouvelé la loi (magistrats) et de tous pris la féauté et hommage, aussi bien comme si il fut comte de Flandres.'

He returns to Ghent and: 'A l'encontre de lui issit (sortit) on a procession et a si grand joie que le comte leur sire en son temps n'y fut point reçu si honorablement comme il fut à ce retour. Et l'adoraient toutes gens comme leur Dieu.'

Froissart also speaks of the abundant provision of his banquets and especially of the sweetmeats.

Again Froissart dwells on the way in which this bourgeois hero takes for himself fine horses: 'Philippe d'Artevelde enchargea un grand état de beaux coursiers et destriers avoir en son séjour, ainsi comme un grand prince.'

So Chaucer refers mockingly to the noble steed of Sir Thopas:

> 'His stede was al dappel-gray,
> It gooth an ambel in the way
> Ful softely and rounde
>   In londe.'

Froissart jests also at the elaborate attire of Philip:

'Et se vêtoit de sanguinis et d'écarlettes et se fourroit de menus vairs, ainsi comme le duc de Brabant ou le comte de Hainaut; et avoit sa chambre aux déniers très riche où on payoit ainsi comme le comte; et donnoit aux dames et aux damoiselles de grands dîners, soupers et banquet, ainsi comme avoit fait du temps passé le comte; et n'épargnoit non plus ni or ni argent que donc que il lui plût des nues.'

Compare this with Chaucer's ironic account of the attire 'of cloth of lake fine and clere,' 'the cote-armour as white as is a lily-flour,' and the magnificent shield 'al of gold so reed.'

We may observe also that Chaucer is quite plainly describing a bourgeois hero because he gives him accomplishments which were the typical accomplishments of the middle-class man but most certainly not of the knight: he is a good archer and a good wrestler and carries away the ram as the prize of a wrestling match; but the bow was not the weapon of the knight, it was the typical weapon of the yeoman and wrestling was also the typical sport of the bourgeoisie; in Chaucer's Prologue it is the miller who is the wrestler and who carries off the ram.

There is also the oath 'by ale and breed' and Froissart makes it one of his chief taunts against the van Arteveldes that the father—Jacques—was a brewer variously described as a brewer of ale or metheglin (*i.e.* beer sweetened with honey); both the ale and the mead are mentioned by Chaucer in connection with Sir Thopas.

Modern historians seem to be agreed that the elder van Artevelde was not a brewer; but it was at any rate the incessant taunt of his enemies. Namèche tells us that the Flamands loved strange animals and creatures from foreign countries, especially parrots, that they kept dogs and falcons and that the court was especially famous for composing plays and tales, many of them on licentious subjects.

So Chaucer mocks at the song of the 'papejay' in the wood; he jeers at the 'grey goshawk' Sir Thopas carried and he tells us that while he was arming his men sang to him:

> 'Of romances that been royales,
> Of popes and of cardinales
> And eek of love-lykinge.'

We can see admirably the sting of ascribing love-romances to the 'popes and cardinals' when we remember that Urban VI blessed Philip van Artevelde and considered his cause as a crusade.

Another minor detail may also be observed. The name of the giant 'Olifaunt' was the name of the great horn of Roland in the *Chanson de Roland*; as such it was symbolic of French chivalry and the army which opposed Philip van Artevelde was almost entirely composed of the French noblesse and their feudal servants for the burghers of the great towns could not be trusted to take any part in the attack.

V

GRAMMAR AND METRE OF CHAUCER

PRONUNCIATION.

Chaucer's pronunciation differed considerably from that of Modern English and his vowels are generally supposed to have had the continental values. They are:

ā   as in *father*.

ă   short variety of the above as in *ăha*.

ē   had two values, close and open; close *ē* as in Fr. *é*, derived from A.S. *ē* or *ēo*, usually appears as *ee* in Mod. English.

> A.S. *swēte*, Ch. *swete*, Mod. English *sweet*.
> A.S. *dēop*, Ch *depe*, Mod. English *deep*.

Open *é* as in Fr. *è*, from A.S. *ĕa* or *ǽ*, usually appears in Mod. English as *ea*.

> A.S. *hǽlan*, Ch. *hele*, Mod. English *heal*.
> A.S. *ĕast*, Ch. *est*, Mod. English *east*.

ĕ   as in Mod. English *bed, tell*, etc.

ī   as in Mod. English *ee* in *feed*. In Chaucer this sound is spelt either *i* or *y*. A.S. *wrītan*, Ch. *write*. A.S. *drīfan*, Ch. *dryve*.

ĭ   as in Fr. *fini*.

ō   has two sounds, close and open. Close *ō* like the *o* in *note* or in German *so*. It comes from A.S. *ō* and is usually represented in Mod. English by *oo*.

> A.S. *bōc*, Ch. *boke*, Mod. English *book*.
> A.S. *rōt*, Ch. *rote*, Mod. English *root*.

Open *ō* like the *au* of *Paul*. It is generally derived from A.S. *ā* and in Mod. English becomes *oa* or *o*.

> A.S. *lār*, Ch. *lore*, Mod. English *lore*.
> A.S. *brād*, Ch. *brode*, Mod. English *broad*.

ŏ   as in *box, hot*. Before *nasals, n, m, ŏ* is sounded as *ŭ*.

> A.S. *munuc*, Ch. *monk*, Mod. English *monk*.

ū   as in *fool* or like Fr. *ou* in *vous*. It is often written *ou* but not pronounced as a diphthong: *flour*.

ŭ   as in *full*.

DIPHTHONGS.

ai, ay, ei, ey as in Mod. English *ay* in *day, way*, etc. Ch. *breyde, brayde, demeine*, etc.

au as in Mod. English *ou* or *ow* in *sound, now*, etc. Ch. *avaunt, faucon*, etc.

oi as in words of French origin like *boil, noise*, etc.

GRAMMAR
NOUNS.

PLURAL. In Chaucer most nouns have conformed to the ordinary masculine declension (A.S. *as* plurals) and take their plural in *es* pronounced as a separate syllable: *naylès, hennès, owlès, wormès, wyvès*, etc.

Occasionally the plural is spelt *is*: *eeris, heeris, beryis*.

Nouns of French origin often form their plural in *s* only: *mirours, jogelours, auctours*, etc.

Chaucer has also relics of A.S. declensions, more numerous than in Mod. English.

NEUTER NOUNS (unchanged for the plural): *sheep, neet, swyn, deer, hors, yeer,* etc.

WEAK NOUNS (taking an *en* plural): *toon*[1]*, foon*[2]*, been*[3]*, oxen, hosen, eyen*[4]*, asshen*[5], etc.

(Some of these have alternative strong forms.)

MUTATION NOUNS (showing vowel change): *goos, gees; fote, fete,* etc.

Some nouns such as *keen (cows)* show a combination of mutation and weak ending.

GENITIVE. In Chaucer the genitive of the noun is usually formed in *es* and pronounced as a separate syllable: *mannès, Goddès, wommennès, senatourès,* etc.

Foreign nouns ending in *s* have sometimes no special form for the genitive: *Venus children.*

In A.S. the class known as *r* nouns took no *s*: so in Chaucer, *fader soule, fader kyn.*

The A.S. fem. genitive ended in *e* and Chaucer has a number of instances: *Nonne Prestes, herte blood, lady grace,* etc.

The genitive plural of the A.S. weak noun ended in *ena* and there seems to be a relic of this in the form: *hevene king.*

DATIVE. Chaucer frequently employs the dative case; it ends in *e* which is pronounced as a separate syllable and occurs regularly after such prepositions as *at, by, in,* etc.: *in londè, in the dawenyngè, in his throtè, by kynde, of hewe,* etc.

ADJECTIVES.

PLURAL. A.S. adjectives varied their plurals in agreement with the nouns but the most common form was in *e* and this is the regular form for the plural in Chaucer: *redè lemès, redè beestès, blakè berès, blakè develès,* etc.

There are occasional though rare examples of a French adjective plural in *s*: *places delitables (Franklin's Tale), romances that been royales (Sir Thopas).*

[1] Toes.   [2] Foes.   [3] Bees.   [4] Eyes.   [5] Ashes.

DEFINITE FORM. The definite form of the adj. is used when the adj. is preceded by the definite article, by a demonstrative or possessive or agrees with a noun in the vocative case: *this fairè Pertelote, deerè brother, this samè nyght*, etc.

COMPARISON. Adjectives are compared by adding *er* or *re* (*derre, ferre*) for the comparative, and *est* for the superlative.

A certain number of adjs. compare by mutation: *old, elder, eldest; long, lengra, lengest; strong, strenger* or *strengra, strengest*.

There are also irregular adjectives:

god	bet	best
yvel	wers	werste
muchel	*mo* or *more*	moste
litel or *lite*	lesse	leeste
(*far*)	fer	ferrest
(*neigh*)	neer	nexte
(*fore*)		firste

ADVERBS.

Adverbs are frequently formed from adjectives by the addition of *e* or *ly*: *trewely, myrily, softè, sorè, loudè, privèly, boldèly*, etc. Adverbs are frequently formed from the genitive.

PRONOUNS.

PERSONAL PRONOUNS:

First Pers. Sing.	*Second Pers. Sing.*
N. I, ich, ik	thou
A. me	thee
D. me	thee
G. my or myn	thy or thyn

(Note.—The second person singular is regularly employed when the person addressed is an inferior or on terms of familiarity.)

First Pers. Plur.	*Second Pers. Plur.*
N. we	ye
A. us	you
D. us	you
G. oure	youre

Third Pers. Sing.

Masc.	Neut.	Fem.
N. he	hit, it	she
A. him	hit, it	hire, hir
D. him	him	hire, hir
G. his	his	hire

Third Pers. Plural.

N. they
A. hem
D. hem
G. here, hir

(Note.—In A.S. all the forms of this pronoun began in *h*; the *th* forms are really of Scandinavian origin; Chaucer only employs the *th* form in the nominative.)

INDEFINITE PRONOUN. Chaucer retains the indef. pronoun *men* (corresponding to French *on* or German *man*); it can be distinguished from the plural of the noun by the fact that it always takes a singular verb: *or if men smoot it.*

DEMONSTRATIVE PRONOUNS. *That* has a plural *tho* (A.S. *þā*): *tho herbes. At the* is often contracted to *atte*: *atte thridde time.*

RELATIVE PRONOUNS. *That* is used for persons as well as for things and is both singular and plural. *Which* has a plural *whiche*.

(Notes.—*ilk* (A.S. *ælc*) means *the same*; *thilke* (A.S. *þe* + *ǣlc*); *swich* (A.S. *swilc*) *such*; *som* (A.S. *sum*) *a* or *an*; plural *some*; *al* (A.S. *eall*), plur. *alle*, gen. plur. *aller* or *alder*; *echoon* (A.S. *ǣlc* + *ān*) *each one*; *everichoon* (A.S. *ǣfre* + *ǣlc* + *ān*) *everyone*.)

VERBS.

In Chaucer there are seven conjugations of strong verbs.

Class I. Verbs with *ī* (Chaucer *ȳ*) infinitive:

	Infin.	Pret. Sing.	Pret. Plur.	P. P.
A.S.	*wrītan*	*wrāt*	*writon*	*writen*
Ch.	*wrȳte*	*wroot*	*writen*	*writen*
	rȳde	*rood*	*riden*	*riden*

Class II. Verbs with *ēo* (Chaucer *ee*) or *ū* infinitive:

	Infin.	Pret. Sing.	Pret. Plur.	P. P.
A.S.	*cēosan*	*cēas*	*curon*	*coren*
Ch.	*cheese*	*chees*	*chosen*	*chosen*

Class III. Verbs with infinitive in *ĕ* or *ĭ* followed by a double consonant:

	Infin.	Pret. Sing.	Pret. Plur.	P. P.
A.S.	*drincan*	*dranc*	*druncon*	*druncen*
A.S.	*helpan*	*healp*	*hulpon*	*holpen*
Ch.	*drinke*	*drank*	*dronken*	*dronken*
	helpe	*halp*	*holpen*	*holpen*

Class IV. Verbs with infinitive in *ĕ* or *ĭ* followed by a single consonant either a liquid or a nasal:

	Infin.	Pret. Sing.	Pret. Plur.	P. P.
A.S.	*beran*	*bær*	*bǣron*	*boren*
Ch.	*bere*	*bar*	*bĕren*	*boren*
	come	*cam* or *coom*	*coomen*	*comen*

Class V. Verbs with infinitive in *ĕ* or *ĭ* followed by a single consonant not a liquid or a nasal:

	Infin.	Pret. Sing.	Pret. Plur.	P. P.
A.S.	*sittan*	*sǣt*	*sǣton*	*seten*
Ch.	*sitte*	*sat, seet*	*seeten, seten*	*seten*

Class VI. Verbs with infinitive in *ă*:

	Infin.	Pret. Sing.	Pret. Plur.	P. P.
A.S.	*scacan*	*scōc*	*scōcon*	*scacen*
Ch.	*shake*	*shook*	*shooken*	*shaken*

Class VII. Verbs originally reduplicating; root vowels various, including *ă, ā, ō, ē*:

	Infin.	Pret. Sing.	Pret. Plur.	P. P.
A.S.	*feallan*	*fēoll*	*fēollon*	*feallen*
A.S.	*grōwan*	*grēow*	*grēowon*	*grōwen*
Ch.	*falle*	*fel, fil*		*fallen*
	growe	*grew*		*growen*

WEAK VERBS. **Class I.** Verbs which employ the stem vowel *e* in adding the pret. and p.p. endings on to the root:

	Infin.	Pret. Sing.	P. P.
A.S.	*derian*	*derede*	*dered*
Ch.	*dere*	*derede*	*dered*

Class II. Verbs which add the pret. and p.p. endings directly on to the root:

DIVISION A. Verbs which have the same vowel in infinitive and preterite:

	Infin.	Pret. Sing.	P. P.
A.S.	*hīeran*	*hīerde*	*hīered*
Ch.	*here*	*herde*	*herd*
	feele	*felte*	*felt*

DIVISION B. Verbs which have a mutated vowel in the infinitive but not in the preterite:

	Infin.	Pret. Sing.	P. P.
A.S.	*sēcean*	*sōhte*	*sōht*
Ch.	*seeken*	*soughte*	*sought*
	tellen	*tolde*	*told*

PRESENT INDICATIVE. The Chaucerian verb has endings for each of the three persons in the singular:

First Pers. *e*   Second Pers. *est*   Third Pers. *eth*

and a common ending for the plural in *en*:

First Pers.	*bere*	*ryde*
Second Pers.	*berest*	*rydest*
Third Pers.	*bereth*	*rydeth* or *rit*
Pl.	*beren*	*ryden*

(Notes.—Verbs which end in a dental often abbreviate the third person: *stant* (*standeth*), *bit* (*biddeth*), *sit* (*sitteth*), etc. The plural *en* is sometimes abbreviated to *e*: *wende* (*wenden*), *pleye* (*pleyen*), *speke* (*speken*).

SUBJUNCTIVE. The subjunctive of the verb takes *e* in the three persons of the singular and *en* in the plural, the latter often abbreviated to *e*.

IMPERATIVE. The imperative singular of strong verbs is formed from the simple root: *tak heed, tel me anon*, etc.

In weak verbs the imperative singular ends in *e*: *shewe now, trille this pin*, etc.

The imperative plural ends in *eth*: *beth pacient, now herkneth*, etc.

INFINITIVE. The simple infinitive ends in *en* or *e*: *dauncen, drenchen, loken, lette, falle*, etc.

The dative infinitive ends in *en* or *e* and takes *to* or *for to* before it: *to goon on pilgrimages, for to seken, for to lighte*, etc.

PARTICIPLES. The present participle ends in *ing* or *inge* (*yng, ynge*). The past participle often has the prefix *y*, A.S. *ge*: *y-seyled, y-passed, y-ronne*, etc.

ANOMALOUS VERBS.

BE Pres. Sing. *am, art, is*; Plur. *been, ben, arn*. Pret. Sing. *was, were, was*; Plur. *weren, were*. Imp. *beeth*. P. P. *been, ben*.

CAN (*I know*) 2nd, 3rd Pers. Sing. *can*; Pl. *connen*. Pt. *coude* (*knew, could*). P. P. *couth* (*known*).

DAR *I dare*. Pt. *dorste*.

MAY *I may*. Pl. *mowen*. Subj. *mowe*.

MOOT *I* or *he must, I* or *he may*. Pl. *moten*. Pt. *moste*.

SHALL *I* or *he shall*. Pl. *shullen*. Pt. *sholde*.

THAR *I* or *he needs*.

WIL *wol, wole*; *I* or *he will*. Pl. *wolen* or *willen*. Pt. *wolde*.

WOOT *wōt*; *I* or *he knows*. Pl. *witen* or *woot*. Pt. *wiste*.

METRE

In his minor poems Chaucer employs a certain number of complex forms: roundels, triple roundels, etc.[1], but in the main portion of his work he employs three different metres; the octosyllabic couplet, the seven-lined stanza, and the decasyllabic couplet.

The octosyllabic couplet was one of the favourite metres of the 14th century; it was employed by Barbour, Gower and many other writers. Chaucer makes use of it mainly in his first period, in his translation of the *Roman de la Rose*, and in the *Book of the Duchesse*, also in one later poem, the *Hous of Fame*.

Chaucer's seven-lined stanza was a metre which had been known before but which he was the first to make popular; it is characteristic of the works composed in

[1] See Introduction I.

his so-called 'Italian period' and he was probably influenced in his choice of it by its similarity to Boccaccio's
'ottava rima.'

The characteristic metre of the *Canterbury Tales* is the
decasyllabic couplet; this was a favourite metre in French
and had been known in English before Chaucer but his
handling of it is so infinitely superior to that of any pre-
decessor that, so far as English literature is concerned,
he may be considered as practically the creator of the
metre which has ever since remained one of the chief
measures of English poetry.

The typical line contains five iambic feet but feminine
rhymes are exceedingly numerous in Chaucer so that
lines of eleven syllables are even commoner than those
of ten; it seems probable that an additional syllable
is allowed at the caesura also and some critics think
trisyllabic feet fairly common in all parts of the line.
Professor Saintsbury believes that Chaucer permits the
use of Alexandrines[1].

A peculiar feature of the heroic line in Chaucer (not
permissible in later English) is that it may omit the first
syllable and thus begin with a strong accent; this not
infrequently results in the line being in trochaic or falling
metre throughout.

We may give some lines as illustrations:

(*a*) Regular iambic:

   'Was lyk an hòund and wòlde han màad areèst.'

(*b*) Eleven-syllabled, with feminine ending:

   'But swich a joy was it to here hem syngë.'

(*c*) With additional syllable at the caesura:

   'What schulde he studie | and make himselven wood.'
   'To Caunterbury | with ful devout corage.'

(*d*) With omission of first syllable and hence in trochaic metre:

   'Twènty bòkes clàd in blàk and reèd.'
   'Fòr to dèlen wìth no swìch poraìllë.'

[1] *History of Prosody*, ii. iv.

(*e*) With reversal of stress in first syllable:
> 'Rìght in the nèxtë chàpitre àfter thìs.'

(*f*) An Alexandrine:
> 'Westward | right swich | another in | the opposite.'

A great deal of the melody of Chaucer's lines depends on the proper treatment of final *e*. Elision is very frequent and takes place in the following cases:

(1) When final *e* is followed by a vowel.

(2) When final *e* is followed by a French word beginning with silent *h* or an English pronoun with an unemphatic *h*: *his, him, hit*, etc.

(3) In frequently occurring verbs such as *come, were, nolde, wolde, have*, the *e* is usually ignored. *Coude* is a difficult form because the *e* is quite irregular, so is *hadde*.

(4) *e* is usually elided in weak syllables followed by a vowel, weak syllables being *er, el, en, ed*, etc.

Examples:

(1) 'But I ne kan nat bulte it to the bren.'
'Ther as he was ful myrie and wel at ese.'
'Certes, it was of herte, al that he song.'

(2) 'And whan that Pertelote thus herde hym rore.'
'Seyde he nat thus "Ne do no fors of dremes."'
'And brende hirselven with a stedefast herte.'

(3) 'By God, I haddë levere than my sherte
That ye hadde red his legende as have I.'
'That he hadde met that dreem that I yow tolde.'
'Than wolde I shewe you how that I koude pleyne.'

(4) 'Swevenes engendren of replecciouns.'
'As for a soverayn notabilitee.'
'So hydous was the noys, a benedicitee.'

THE PRIORESS'S TALE

AND

THE TALE OF SIR THOPAS

CANTERBURY TALES

THE PROLOGE OF THE PRIORESSES TALE

Domine dominus noster

O lord oure lord, thy name how merueillous
Is in this large world ysprad—quod she—
ffor noght oonly thy laude precious
Parfourned is by men of dignitee,
But by the mouth of children thy bountee   5
Parfourned is, for on the brest soukynge
Somtyme shewen they thyn heriynge.

Wherfore in laude, as I best kan or may,
Of thee, and of the white[1] lylye flour
Which that the bar, and is a mayde alway,   10
To telle a storie I wol do my labour;
Nat that I may encreessen hir honour;
ffor she hir self is honour, and the roote
Of bountee, next hir sone, and soules boote.—

O mooder mayde! o mayde mooder fre!   15
O bussh vnbrent, brennynge in Moyses sighte,
That rauysedest doun fro the deitee,
Thurgh thyn humblesse, the goost that in thalighte,
Of whos vertu, whan he thyn herte lighte,
Conceyued was the fadres sapience,   20
Helpe me to telle it in thy reuerence!

[1] Hengwrt MS.

Lady! thy bountee, thy magnificence,
Thy vertu, and thy grete humylitee
Ther may no tonge expresse in no science;
ffor somtyme, lady, er men praye to thee,   25
Thou goost biforn of thy benygnytee[1],
And getest vs thurgh lyght of thy preyere
To gyden vs vn to thy sone so deere.

My konnyng is so wayk, o blisful queene,
ffor to declare thy grete worthynesse,   30
That I ne may the weighte nat susteene,
But as a child of twelf monthe oold, or lesse,
That kan vnnethe any word expresse,
Right so fare I, and therfore I yow preye,
Gydeth my song that I shal of yow seye.   35

Explicit

HEERE BIGYNNETH THE PRIORESSES TALE

Ther was in Asye, in a greet Citee,
Amonges cristene folk, a Iewerye,
Sustened by a lord of that contree
ffor foule vsure and lucre of vileynye,
Hateful to Crist and to his compaignye,   40
And thurgh the strete men myghte ride or wende,
ffor it was free, and open at eyther ende.

A litel scole of cristen folk ther stood
Doun at the ferther ende, in which ther were
Children an heepe, ycomen of cristen blood,   45
That lerned in that scole yeer by yere
Swich manere doctrine as men vsed there,
This is to seyn, to syngen and to rede,
As smale children doon in hire childhede.

[1] Hengwrt.

Among thise children was a wydwes sone,   50
A litel clergeon, seuen yeer of age,
That day by day to scole was his wone,
And eek also, where as he saugh thymage
Of Cristes mooder, he hadde in vsage
As hym was taught, to knele adoun and seye   55
His Aue Marie, as he goth by the weye.

Thus hath this wydwe hir litel sone ytaught
Oure blisful lady, cristes mooder deere,
To worshipe ay, and he forgate it naught;
ffor sely child wol alday soone leere;   60
But ay, whan I remembre on this mateere,
Seint Nicholas stant euere in my presence,
ffor he so yong to Crist dide reuerence.

This litel child, his litel book lernynge,
As he sat in the scole at his prymer,   65
He Alma redemptoris herde synge,
As children lerned hire Antiphoner[1];
And as he dorste, he drough hym ner and ner,
And herkned ay the wordes and the noote,
Til he the firste vers koude al by rote.   70

Noght wiste he what this latyn was to seye,
ffor he so yong and tendre was of age;
But on a day his felawe gan he preye
Texpounden hym this song in his langage,
Or telle hym why this song was in vsage;   75
This preyde he hym to construe and declare
fful often tyme vpon hise knowes bare.

His felawe which that elder was than he
Answerde hym thus: 'this song, I haue herd seye,

[1] Hengwrt.

Was maked of oure blisful lady free,   80
Hire to salue, and eek hire for to preye
To been oure help and socour whan we deye.
I kan na moore expounde in this mateere;
I lerne song, I kan but smal grammeere.'

'And is this song maked in reuerence   85
Of Cristes mooder?' seyde this Innocent;
'Now certes, I wol do my diligence
To konne it al, er Cristemasse is went;
Though that I for my prymer shal be shent,
And shal be beten thriës in an houre,   90
I wol it konne, oure lady for to honoure.'

His felawe taughte hym homward priuely,
ffro day to day, til he koude it by rote,
And thanne he song it wel and boldely
ffro word to word, acordynge with the note[1];   95
Twiës a day it passed thurgh his throte,
To scoleward and homward whan he wente;
On Cristes mooder set was his entente.

As I haue seyd, thurgh out the Iuerie
This litel child, as he cam to and fro,   100
fful murily wolde he synge, and crie
O Alma redemptoris euere mo.
The swetnesse his herte perced so
Of Cristes mooder, that, to hire to preye,
He kan nat stynte of syngyng by the weye.   105

Ovre firstè foo, the serpent Sathanas,
That hath in Iues herte his waspes nest,
Vp swal, and seide, 'o. Hebrayk peple, allas!
Is this to yow a thyng that is honest,

[1] Hengwrt.

That swich a boy shal walken as hym lest   110
In youre despit, and synge of swich sentence,
Which is agayn oure lawes reuerence?'

ffro thennes forth the Iues han conspired
This Innocent out of this world to chace;
An homycide ther to han they hyred,   115
That in an aleye hadde a priuee place;
And as the child gan forby for to pace,
This cursed Iew hym hente and heeld hym faste,
And kitte his throte, and in a pit hym caste.

I seye that in a wardrobe they hym threwe   120
Where as thise Iewes purgen hire entraille.
O cursed folk of Herodes al newe,
What may youre yuel entente yow auaille?
Mordre wol out, certeyn, it wol nat faille,
And namely ther thonour of god shal sprede,   125
The blood out crieth on youre cursed dede.

'O martir, sowded to virginitee,
Now maystow syngen, folwynge euere in oon
The white lamb celestial,' quod she,
'Of which the grete Euaungelist, Seint Iohn   130
In Pathmos wroot, which seith that they that goon
Biforn this lamb, and synge a song al newe,
That neuere, fleshly, wommen they ne knewe.'

This poure wydwe awaiteth al that nyght
After hir litel child, but he cam noght;   135
ffor which as soone as it was dayes lyght,
With face pale of drede and bisy thoght,
She hath at scole and elles where hym soght,
Til finally she gan so fer espie
That he last seyn was in the Iuerie.   140

With moodres pitee in hir brest enclosed,
She gooth, as she were half out of hir mynde,
To euery place where she hath supposed
By liklihede hir litel child to fynde;
And euere on Cristes mooder meeke and kynde   145
She cride, and atte laste thus she wroghte,
Among the cursed Iues she hym soghte.

She frayneth and she preyeth pitously
To euery Iew that dwelte in thilke place,
To telle hire if hir child wente oght forby.   150
They seyde 'nay'; but Ihesu, of his grace,
Yaf in hir thoght, inwith a litel space,
That in that place after hir sone she cryde,
Where he was casten in a pit bisyde.

O grete god, that parfournest thy laude   155
By mouth of Innocentz, lo heere thy myght!
This gemme of chastite, this Emeraude,
And eek of martirdom the Ruby bright,
Ther he with throte ykoruen lay vpright,
He 'Alma redemptoris' gan to synge   160
So loude, that al the place gan to rynge.

The cristene folk, that thurgh the strete wente,
In coomen, for to wondre vp on this thyng,
And hastily they for the Prouost sente;
He cam anon with outen tariyng,   165
And herieth Crist that is of heuene kyng,
And eek his mooder, honour of mankynde,
And after that, the Iewes leet he bynde.

This child with pitous lamentacion
Vp taken was, syngynge his song alway;   170

And with honour of greet procession
They carien hym vn to the nexte Abbay.
His mooder swownynge by his beere lay;
Vnnethe myghte the peple that was theere
This newe Rachel brynge fro his beere.   175

With torment and with shameful deeth echon
This Prouost dooth the Iewes for to sterue
That of this mordre wiste, and that anon;
He nolde no swich cursednesse obserue.
Yuele shal he haue, that yuele wol deserue.   180
Therfore with wilde hors he dide hem drawe,
And after that he heng hem by the lawe.

Vp on this beere ay lith this Innocent
Biforn the chief Auter, whil the masse laste,
And after that, the Abbot with his Couent   185
Han sped hem for to burien hym ful faste;
And whan they hooly water on hym caste,
Yet spak this child, whan spreynd was hooly water,
And song—'O Alma redemptoris mater!'

This Abbot, which that was an hooly man   190
As Monkes been, or elles oghte be,
This yonge child to coniure he bigan,
And seyde, 'o deere child, I halse thee,
In vertu of the hooly Trinitee,
Tel me what is thy cause for to synge,   195
Sith that thy throte is kut, to my semynge?'

'My throte is kut vn to my nekke boon,'
Seyde this child, 'and, as by wey of kynde,
I sholde haue dyed, ye, longe tyme agon,
But Ihesu Crist, as ye in bookes fynde,   200
Wil that his glorie laste and be in mynde,

And, for the worship of his mooder deere,
Yet may I synge "O Alma" loude and cleere.

This welle of mercy, Cristes mooder sweete,
I loued alwey, as after my konnynge;   205
And whan that I my lyf sholde forlete,
To me she cam and bad me for to synge
This Antheme[1] verraily in my deyynge,
As ye han herd, and whan that I hadde songe,
Me thoughte, she leyde a greyn vp on my tonge.   210

Wherfore I synge, and synge I moot certeyn
In honour of that blisful mayden free,
Til fro my tonge of taken is the greyn;
And afterward thus seyde she to me,
"My litel child, now wol I fecche thee   215
Whan that the greyn is fro thy tonge ytake;
Be nat agast, I wol thee nat forsake."'

This hooly Monk, this Abbot, hym meene I,
His tonge out caughte, and took a-wey the greyn
And he yaf vp the goost ful softely.   220
And whan this Abbot hadde this wonder seyn,
Hise salte teeris trikled doun as reyn,
And gruf he fil al plat vp on the grounde,
And stille he lay as he had leyn ybounde.

The Couent eek lay on the pauement   225
Wepynge, and heryen cristes mooder deere,
And after that they ryse, and forth been went,
And tooken awey this martir from his beere,
And in a temple of Marbul stones cleere
Enclosen they his litel body sweete;   230
Ther he is now god leue us for to meete[2].

[1] Hengwrt.   [2] Id.

O yonge Hugh of Lyncoln, slayn also
With cursed Iewes, as it is notable,
ffor it is but a litel while ago;
Preye eek for vs, we synful folk vnstable,   235
That, of his mercy, god so merciable
On vs his grete mercy multiplie,
ffor reuerence of his mooder Marie.   Amen.

Heere is ended the Prioresses Tale.

BIHOOLD THE MURYE WORDES OF THE HOOST TO CHAUCER

Whan seyd was al this miracle, euery man
As sobre was, that wonder was to se,   240
Til that oure hoost Iapen to bigan,
And thanne at erst he looked vp on me,
And seyde thus, 'what man artow?' quod he?
'Thou lookest as thou woldest fynde an hare
ffor euere vp on the ground I se thee stare.   245

Approche neer, and looke vp murily.
Now war yow, sires, and lat this man haue place;
He in the waast is shape as wel as I.
This were a popet in an Arm tenbrace
ffor any womman, smal and fair of face.   250
He semeth eluyssh by his contenance,
ffor vn to no wight dooth he daliance.

Sey now somwhat, syn oother folk han sayd;
Telle vs a tale of myrthe, and that anon;'—
'Hoost,' quod I, 'ne beth nat yuele apayd,   255
ffor oother tale certes kan I noon,

But of a rym I lerned longe agoon.'
'Ye, that is good,' quod he; 'now shul ye heere
Som deyntee thyng, me thynketh by his cheere.'

Explicit

HEERE BIGYNNETH CHAUCERS TALE OF THOPAS

[*The First Fit*]

[*Each third line is on the right of its couple, in the MS.*]

Listeth, lordes, in good entent   260
And I wol telle verrayment
   Of myrthe and of solas;
Al of a knyght was fair and gent
In bataille and in tourneyment,
   His name was sire Thopas.   265

Yborn he was in fer contree,
In Flaundres, al biyonde the see,
   At Poperyng in the place;
His fader was a man ful free,
And lord he was of that contree,   270
   As it was goddes grace.

Sire Thopas wax a doghty swayn,
Whit was his face as Payndemayn,
   Hise lippes rede as rose;
His rode is lyk scarlet in grayn,   275
And I yow telle in good certayn,
   He hadde a semely nose.

His heer, his berd was lyk saffroun,
That to his girdel raughte adoun;
   Hise shoos of Cordewane.   280
Of Brugges were his hosen broun,
His Robe was of Syklatoun,
   That coste many a Iane.

He koude hunte at wilde deer,
And ride an haukyng for Riuer,   285
   With grey goshauk on honde.
Ther-to he was a good Archeer,
Of wrastlyng was ther noon his peer,
   Ther any Ram shal stonde.

fful many a mayde, bright in bour,   290
They moorne for hym, paramour,
   Whan hem were bet to slepe;
But he was chaast and no lechour,
And sweete as is the Brembul-flour
   That bereth the rede hepe.   295

And so bifel vp on a day,
ffor sothe, as I yow telle may,
   Sire Thopas wolde out ride;
He worth vpon his steede gray,
And in his hand a launcegay,   300
   A long swerd by his side.

He priketh thurgh a fair forest,
Ther Inne is many a wilde best,
   Ye, bothe bukke and hare;
And as he priketh North and Est,   305
I telle it yow, hym hadde almest
   Bitidde a sory care.

Ther spryngen herbes grete and smale,
The lycorys and Cetewale,
    And many a clowe gylofre;   310
And Notemuge to putte in Ale,
Wheither it be moyste or stale,
    Or for to leye in cofre.

The briddes synge, it is no nay,
The sparhauk and the papeiay,   315
    That ioye it was to heere;
The thrustelcok made eek hir lay,
The wodedowue vp on a spray
    She sang ful loude and cleere.

Sire Thopas fil in loue longynge   320
Al whan he herde the thrustel synge,
    And pryked as he were wood:
His faire steede in his prikynge
So swatte that men myghte him wrynge,
    His sydes were al blood.   325

Sire Thopas eek so wery was
ffor prikyng on the softe gras,
    So fiers was his corage,
That doun he leyde him in that plas
To make his steede som solas,   330
    And yaf hym good forage.

'O seinte Marie, benedicite!
What eyleth this loue at me
    To bynde me so soore?
Me dremed al this nyght, pardee,   335
An elf queene shal my lemman be,
    And slepe vnder my goore.

An Elf queene wol I loue, ywis,
ffor in this world no womman is
   Worthy to be my make?   340
         In towne
Alle othere wommen I forsake,
And to an Elf queene I me take
   By dale and eek by downe.'

In to his sadel he clamb anon,   345
And priketh ouer stile and stoon
   An Elf queene for tespye,
Til he so longe hadde riden and goon
That he foond in a pryue woon,
   The contree of ffairye   350
         so wilde;
ffor in that contree was ther noon?
[. . . . *no gap in the MS.*]
   Neither wyf ne childe

Til that ther cam a greet geaunt,
His name was sire Olifaunt,   355
   A perilous man of dede;
He seyde, 'child, by Termagaunt,
But if thou prike out of myn haunt,
   Anon I sle thy steede
         with mace.   360
Heere is the queene of ffairye,
With harpe and pipe and symphonye
   Dwellynge in this place.'

The child seyde, 'Al so moote I thee,
Tomorwe wol I meete with thee   365
   Whan I haue myn Armoure;

And yet I hope, par ma fay,
That thou shalt with this launcegay
   Abyen it ful sowre;
              Thy mawe   370
Thyn hauberk, shal I percen, if I may,
Er it be fully pryme of day,
   ffor heere thow shalt be slawe.'

Sire Thopas drow abak ful faste;
This geant at hym stones caste   375
   Out of a fel staf-slynge;
But faire escapeth sire Thopas,
And al it was thurgh goddes gras,
   And thurgh his fair berynge.

Yet listeth, lordes, to my tale   380
Murier than the Nightyngale,
   I wol yow rowne
How sir Thopas with sydes smale,
Prikyng ouer hill and dale,
   Is comen agayn to towne.   385

His murie men comanded he
To make hym bothe game and glee,
   ffor nedes moste he fighte
With a geaunt with heuedes three,
ffor paramour and Iolitee   390
   Of oon that shoon ful brighte.

'Do come,' he seyde, 'my Mynstrales,
And geestours, for to tellen tales
   Anon in myn Armynge;
Of Romances that been Roiales,   395
Of Popes and of Cardinales,
   And eek of loue likynge.'

They sette hym first sweete wyn,
And Mede eek in a Mazelyn,
 And Roial spicerye;   400
And Gyngebreed that was ful fyn,
And lycorys, and eek Comyn,
 With sugre that is so trye.

He dide next his white leere
Of clooth of lake fyn and cleere   405
 A breech and eek a sherte;
And next his sherte an Aketon,
And ouer that an haubergeon
 ffor percynge of his herte;

And ouer that a fyn hawberk,   410
Was al ywroght of Iewes werk,
 fful strong it was of plate;
And ouer that his cote Armour
As whit as is a lilye flour,
 In which he wol debate.   415

His sheeld was al of gold so reed,
And ther Inne was a bores heed,
 A Charbocle bisyde;
And there he swoor, on ale and breed,
How that 'the geaunt shal be deed, 420
 Bityde what bityde!'

Hise Iambeux were of quyrboilly,
His swerdes shethe of Yuory,
 His helm of laton bright;
His sadel was of Rewel boon,   425
His brydel as the sonne shoon,
 Or as the moone light.

His spere it was of fyn Ciprees,
That bodeth werre, and no thyng pees,
  The heed ful sharpe ygrounde;   430
His steede was al dappull gray,
It gooth an Ambil in the way
  fful softely and rounde

        In londe.
Loo, lordes myne, heere is a fit!   435
If ye wol any moore of it,
  To telle it wol I fonde.

        [*The Second Fit*]

Now holde youre mouth, par charitee,
Bothe knyght and lady free,
  And herkneth to my spelle;   440
Of batailles and of Chiualry,
And of ladyes loue drury
  Anon I wol yow telle.

Men speken of Romances of prys,
Of Hornchild and of Ypotys   445
  Of Beves and of sir Gy,
Of sir lybeux and pleyn damour;
But sir Thopas, he bereth the flour
  Of Roial Chiualry.

His goode Steede al he bistrood,   450
And forth vpon his wey he rood
  As sparcle out of the bronde;
Vp on his Creest He bar a tour
And ther Inne stiked a lilie flour,
  God shilde his cors fro shonde!   455

And for he was a knyght Auntrous,
He nolde slepen in noon hous,
   But liggen in his hoode;
His brighte helm was his wonger,
And by hym baiteth his dextrer   460
   Of herbes fyne and goode.

Hym self drank water of the well,
As dide the knyght sire Percyuell,
   So worthy vnder wede,
Til on a day   465

HEERE THE HOOST STYNTETH CHAUCER
OF HIS TALE OF THOPAS

'Na moore of this for goddes dignitee,'
Quod oure hoost, 'for thou makest me
So wery of thy verray lewednesse
That, also wisly god my soule blesse,
Min eres aken of thy drasty speche;   470
Now swich a Rym the deuel I biteche!
This may wel be Rym dogerel,' quod he.
'Why so?' quod I, 'why wiltow lette me
Moore of my tale than another man,
Syn that it is the beste tale I kan?'   475
'By god,' quod he, 'for pleynly, at a word,
Thy drasty rymyng is nat worth a toord;
Thou doost noght elles but despendest tyme,
Sire, at o word, thou shalt no lenger ryme.
Lat se wher thou kanst tellen aught in geeste, 480
Or telle in prose somwhat at the leeste
In which ther be som murthe or som doctryne.'
'Gladly,' quod I, 'by goddes sweete pyne,

I wol yow telle a litel thyng in prose,
That oghte liken yow, as I suppose,   485
Or elles, certes, ye been to daungerous.
It is a moral tale vertuous,
Al be it take somtyme in sondry wyse
Of sondry folk, as I shal yow deuyse.
As thus; ye woot that euery Euaungelist   490
That telleth vs the peyne of Ihesu Crist,
Ne seith nat alle thyng as his felawe dooth,
But nathelees, hir sentence is al sooth,
And alle acorden as in hire sentence,
Al be ther in hir tellyng difference.   495
ffor somme of hem seyn moore, and somme seyn lesse,
Whan they his pitous passioun expresse;
I meene of Mark, Mathew, Luc and Iohn;
But doutelees hir sentence is all oon.
Therfore lordynges alle, I yow biseche,   500
If that yow thynke I varie as in my speche,
As thus, though that I telle som what moore
Of prouerbes, than ye han herd bifoore,
Comprehended in this litel tretys heere,
To enforce with theffect of my mateere,   505
And though I nat the same wordes seye
As ye han herd, yet to yow alle I preye,
Blameth me nat; for as in my sentence,
Shul ye nowher fynden difference
ffro the sentence of this tretys lyte   510
After the which this murye tale I write.
And therfore herkneth what that I shal seye,
And lat me tellen al my tale, I preye.'

Explicit

NOTES

PROLOGUE TO THE PRIORESSES TALE

1. **O lord, oure lord…**: Ps. viii.; the Vulgate version has 'Domine Dominus noster, quam admirabile est nomen tuum in universa terra. Quoniam elevata est magnificentia tua super cœlos: Ex ore infantium et lactentium perfecisti laudem.'

7. **heriynge**: praise. A.S. 'herian,' to praise, 'heriung,' praise.

9. **white lylye flour**: the white lily was the emblem of Mary as is shown in so many pictures of the Annunciation. All white flowers were considered as sacred to the Virgin, but the lily in particular.

11, 12. **laboùr, honoùr**: the accent falls, as is the French fashion, on the second syllable which is very often the case with Chaucer.

14. **soules boote**: literally, 'the remedy for souls,' i.e. the help and profit for souls.

15. **fre**: generous, a very common meaning for the adjective in Chaucerian English.

16. **bussh unbrent**: the burning bush of Moses, which was in flames yet remained unconsumed, was a generally accepted mediaeval image for the Virgin.

17. **That ravysedest**: who didst ravish down.

18. **the goost that in thalighte**: the ghost (i.e. spirit) that alighted in thee. A.S. 'gāst,' breath, spirit or soul.

19. **Of whos vertu**: from whose power.

whan he thyn herte lighte: when He illuminated thy heart. 'Lighte' may be taken either in the sense of lightened thy heart, i.e. made it less melancholy, or illuminated thy heart, i.e. filled it with light.

20. **the fadres sapience**: the wisdom of the Father, i.e. the Son.

21. **in thy reverence**: in such a way that it contributes to show reverence for thee.

24. **in no science**: with however great a degree of knowledge it may be gifted, no tongue can express it; 'science' has the general sense of knowledge. L. 'scientia.'

26. **Thou goost biforn of thy benygnytee**: the Virgin's graciousness even forestalls the prayer of the believer and is,

as it were, beforehand with the entreaty. The idea is taken from Dante, *Paradiso*, XXXIII:

           'La tua benignità non pur soccorre
           A chi dimanda, ma molte fiate
           Liberamente al dimandar precorre.'

29. **konnyng:** cunning, i.e. power; we still employ the word in the same sense when we speak of the 'cunning hand' of the artist or sculptor.

30. **worthynesse:** honour and dignity.

33. **unnethe:** hardly, or scarcely. A.S. 'unēaþe,' uneasily, or with difficulty.

35. **Gydeth:** imperat. plural form, 'guide my song.'

THE PRIORESSES TALE

36. **Asye:** Asia Minor, associated with the Crusades. See Introduction.

37. **a Iewerye:** a Ghetto. In most cities there was a special Jews' quarter, sometimes within and sometimes outside the walls.

39. **ffor foule usure and lucre of vileynye:** for the sake of foul usury and wicked lucre; the Jews were the great usurers of the Middle Ages and for this reason were generally supported by the feudal lords. See Introduction.

42. **ffor it was free:** the street was not a '*cul de sac*' but a thoroughfare, open at both ends.

45. **Children an heepe:** a heap of children, i.e. a large number of children; the idiom is still possible in various dialects of modern English.

47. **Swich manere doctrine:** such kinds of teaching.

48. **to syngen and to rede:** the school was not a full Grammar School, but was a chorister's school only. See Introduction.

51. **clergeon:** a choir-boy or chorister who studied music and reading.

52. **to scole was his wone:** it was his custom to go to school every day. A.S. 'wunian,' to dwell, to be accustomed.

56. **Ave Marie:** the Latin prayer to the Virgin which commenced with these words: 'Ave Maria, gratia plena.'

60. **ffor sely child wol alday soone leere:** for an innocent or good child will always learn easily. A.S. 'gesǣlig,' happy, prosperous.

62. **Seint Nicholas stant:** 'stant' is the abbreviated form

of 'standeth,' the 3rd pers. sing. of the verb 'to stand.'
Saint Nicholas was the patron saint of schoolboys. His legend
tells how, amusingly enough, while he was still a child at the
breast he refused his nourishment on Fridays.

66. **Alma redemptoris:** there were several Latin hymns
commencing with this phrase. One runs:

> 'Alma redemptoris mater,
> quam de caelis misit pater
> propter salutem gentium, etc., etc.'

67. **Antiphoner:** the song-book which contained both words
and music.

70. **koude al by rote:** knew all by heart.

71. **was to seye:** what was the meaning.

74. **Texpounden hym:** to explain to him.

77. **upon hise knowes bare:** upon his bare knees. A.S.
'cnēow,' knee.

84. **I kan but smal grammeere:** I know but little grammar, i.e. he knew but little Latin; the choristers' school only
taught 'song' and reading in English; it was the higher or
Grammar School which taught Latin.

87. **do my diligence:** do my best.

89. **for my prymer shal be shent:** shall be scolded for
neglecting my primer; 'shent' means literally 'spoilt.'

97. **To scoleward and homward:** on the way to school
and on the way home; 'ward' shows direction from. Cp. *The
Prologue*:

> 'Fro Burdeuxward whil that the Chapman sleepe,'

i.e. the Shipman stole wine on the way home from Bordeaux
while the merchant in charge of it slept.

98. **set was his entente:** his whole attention (i.e. his whole
heart) was set on Christ's mother.

105. **He kan nat stynte of syngyng:** he cannot cease from
singing.

106. **the serpent Sathanas:** alluding, of course, to the
Genesis story; in mediaeval illustrations the serpent who
tempts Eve is very often represented as possessed of a human
face.

107. **his waspes nest:** the Jew's heart is as full of malice
as a wasp's nest.

108. **Up swal:** swelled up.

109. **that is honest:** that is honourable.

110. **as hym lest:** as it pleases him. The A.S. verb 'lystan'
is impersonal and takes the dative, and the usage survives in
Middle English.

111. **of swich sentence:** of such meaning. Cp. *The Pro-*

logue concerning the Clerk of Oxford, when his speech is said to be 'schort and quyk and ful of hy sentence,' i.e. full of lofty meaning.

112. **Which is agayn oure lawes reverence:** the hymn sung by the Christian boy is incompatible with the reverence you feel for your law.

118. **hym hente:** seized upon him, laid hold upon him. A.S. 'hentan,' to pursue.

120. **wardrobe:** a privy.

124–5. **Mordre wol out...**
And namely ther thonour of god shal sprede.
Murder will certainly be revealed and made manifest and especially where the honour of God can be shown in such revelation. Cp. also *The Nun's Priest's Tale*:

> 'Mordre wol out, that se we day by day;
> Mordre is so wlatsom, and abhomynable
> To God, that is so just and resonable,
> That he wol nat suffre it heled be.'

127. **sowded to virginitee:** inseparably bound or united to virginity.

128. **evere in oon:** always in the same way.

129. **white lamb celestial:** the use of one adjective (English fashion) before the noun and another (French fashion) after it is a very common idiom in Chaucer and it has ever since remained as an ornament in English poetry. It is one of many examples which show how the double origin of the English language has enriched its resources.

135. **After hir litel child:** for her little child.

137. **pale of drede:** pale through or because of her dread.

139. **so fer espie:** to find out or discover.

146. **thus she wroghte:** she wrought or did thus.

148. **frayneth:** asks or enquires. A.S. 'frignan,' to ask or enquire.

149. **in thilke place:** in that place. A.S. 'þe + ǣlc.'

150. **wente oght forby:** had passed by at all.

152. **Yaf in hir thoght:** suggested to her mind.
inwith: within.

155. **parfournest thy laude:** dost perform thy praise.

159. **lay upright:** full length. This curious idiom was quite common. Cp. *The Nun's Priest's Tale*:

> 'And in this carte he lyeth gapȳnge upright.'

165. **anon:** immediately; literally, 'in one moment.'

168. **leet he bynde:** he caused the Jews to be bound.

174. **Unnethe:** scarcely, or hardly. A.S. 'unēaþe.'

176. **echon:** each one.

177. **dooth the Iewes for to sterve:** causes the Jews to be put to death.

178. **wiste:** knew.

181. **wilde hors:** wild horses. Cp. *The Prologue*, ' His hors weren goode,' where also ' hors' is treated as a plural.

182. **heng hem by the lawe:** caused them to be hanged as the law decreed.

185. **Covent:** convent or monastery of monks.

186. **Han sped hem:** hastened.

188. **spreynd:** sprinkled.

193. **I halse thee:** I entreat or implore thee. A.S. 'hālsian,' conjure or exorcise.

198. **by wey of kynde:** in the natural course of things; ' kynde' means nature.

199. **longe tyme agon:** a long time ago.

205. **after my konnynge:** according to my ability or power.

206. **forlete:** leave. A.S. 'forlǣtan,' to leave or abandon.

211. **synge I moot certeyn:** I must certainly sing; ' mōt' is a preterite present verb.

212. **mayden free:** generous maiden.

217. **Be nat agast:** do not be afraid. Cp. *The Knight's Tale*:

'Ne how the ground agast was of the light.'

223. **gruf he fil al plat up on the grounde:** he fell grovelling and flat on the ground, a use of two words, one in English and one in French, meaning practically the same thing.

229. **Marbul stones cleere:** bright or shining marble; this use of ' cleere' is probably suggested by the use of the Italian adjective ' chiaro.'

231. **Ther he is now god leve us for to meete:** where he is now may God permit us to meet him.

232. **Hugh of Lyncoln:** whose tale showed the closest similarities to the story above. See Introduction.

235. **unstable:** uncertain, changeable.

PROLOGUE TO SIR THOPAS

241. **Iapen:** to jest.

243. **what man artow:** what man art thou? To run the verb and pronoun together was a common idiom in Middle English.

249. **a popet:** a puppet or a doll.

251. **elvyssh:** elf-like or fairy-like, the meaning being that he was strange and reserved in his manners.

252. **un to no wight dooth he daliance:** for he dallies with no one, i.e. he does not toy or make fun with anyone.

255. **ne beth nat yvele apayd:** don't take it amiss. 'Beth' is the imperat. plural form.

256. **certes:** certainly or equally.

259. **Som deyntee thyng:** some delightful thing.

SIR THOPAS

260. **Listeth:** listen, the imperat. plural form.

261. **verrayment:** Fr. 'vraiment,' truly.

262. **Of myrthe and of solas:** a tale of mirth and solace, i.e. a merry tale that will cheer people.

263. **fair and gent:** beautiful and accomplished. The meaning of words in *Sir Thopas* must not be pressed too closely as many of them are meant simply as rhyming tags and many of them are intentionally absurd.

265. **sire Thopas:** no doubt alluding to 'topaz' the jewel and meaning 'a gem of a knight,' but not too valuable a gem.

268. **in the place:** in the principal house in the town.

272. **wax:** grew. A.S. 'weaxan,' to grow.

a doghty swayn: a valiant man. A.S. 'swān,' swineherd or herdsman.

273. **Payndemayn:** the finest white bread. Lat. 'panis Dominicus'; it was a kind of bread specially made for church festivals.

275. **rode:** complexion; literally, ruddy colour.

scarlet in grayn: scarlet dye or cochineal, so-called because of the grain-like appearance of the colour.

278. **lyk saffroun:** coloured a brilliant yellow, like saffron; this, of course, like the rest of the description of the knight's beauties, is purposely absurd.

279. **raughte adoun:** reached down.

280. **Cordewane:** Cordova leather.

282. **Syklatoun:** a costly kind of thin cloth, used also as a material for tents and banners and probably of Eastern origin; the word appears to have been originally the same as 'scarlet.'

283. **many a Iane:** a coin of Genoa: a silver coin of small value.

285. **for River:** along the river-bank where the water-fowl would naturally be found and which therefore provided the best hawking.

286. **on honde:** the hawk was regularly carried on its master's wrist, on a little leather band closely fitted for the purpose.

289. **any Ram:** the ram was the regular prize for wrestling. Cp. *The Prologue*:

'At wrastlynge he wolde have awey the ram,'

in the passage which describes the Miller.

299. **worth upon his steede gray:** he got on his grey horse or steed. A.S. 'weorþan,' to happen, to become.

300. **a launcegay:** a kind of lance.

305. **priketh North and Est:** he rides north-east; pricking refers to the spurring of the rider.

307. **Bitidde a sory care:** a great misfortune had almost happened to him.

309. **Cetewale:** setwall or zedoary; an aromatic plant from the East Indies, used in medicine.

310. **clowe gylofre:** clove, the spice so-called. Fr. 'clou de girofle.'

312. **moyste or stale:** new or old.

313. **to leye in cofre:** for the sake of the scent.

314. **it is no nay:** there is no denial.

315. **the papeiay:** popinjay or green woodpecker.

322. **as he were wood:** rode as if he were mad. A.S. 'wōd,' mad, frenzied.

334. **To bynde me so soore?:** why does love put such bonds upon me? i.e. so sorely oppress me.

336. **lemman:** lady-love.

337. **under my goore:** under my robe. A.S. 'gār,' the spear-shaped inset in the side of a robe and so the robe itself.

338. **ywis:** certainly, truly. A.S. 'gewiss,' certainly.

340. **my make:** my mate. A.S. 'gemaca,' one of a pair, especially a male and female animal, a husband or wife.

344. **by downe:** by the hill. A.S. 'dūn,' hill, mountain or down.

349. **in a pryve woon:** in a secret dwelling-place. A.S. 'wunian,' to dwell or remain, 'wunung,' dwelling.

350. **ffairye:** this is really a collective noun, the country of 'fairye' meaning the country of the fairies.

355. **sire Olifaunt:** Sir Elephant, a burlesque name for the giant.

356. **A perilous man of dede:** a man whose deeds are great and perilous to others.

357. **child:** a general term for a knight, meaning literally a young person.

by Termagaunt: generally supposed in Chaucer's time to be a Mohammedan deity, for Mohammedans were commonly spoken of as if they were idolaters, ignoring the fact that they were strict monotheists. The meaning of the name appears to be Trivigante or Diana Trivia, Diana under her three aspects.

358. **out of myn haunt:** away from my dwelling-place.

359. **I sle thy steede:** to kill a horse was regarded as a particularly unchivalrous and unknightly deed.

362. **symphonye:** a kind of tabor.

364. **Al so moote I thee:** as I may thrive. A.S. 'þēon,' to thrive, be prosperous or successful.

369. **Abyen it ful sowre:** pay for it very sorely.

372. **pryme of day:** nine o'clock; the day was divided into four periods of three hours each, the first of which, from 6 a.m. to 9 a.m., was known as 'pryme'; 'fully pryme' means the end of this period or nine o'clock.

380. **listeth:** listen, imperat. plural form.

382. **yow rowne:** whisper or say to you. A.S. 'rūnian,' whisper or mutter.

390. **ffor paramour and Iolitee:** for the love and pleasure of his lady.

392. **Do come:** cause to come or make to come.

393. **geestours:** the narrators of tales; the 'chansons de geste' were epic tales told in verse and these were narrated by travelling tale-tellers or 'gestours.'

394. **Anon in myn Armynge:** he wants the 'gestours' to tell him tales whilst his armour was put on.

395. **Romances that been Roiales:** romances dealing with royalty; this is an exceptionally interesting idiom and the only example of its kind in Chaucer, for it shows alike the French position of the adjective after the copula and the French plural of the adjective in 's.'

399. **Mede:** the drink so-called, made largely from honey and spiced.

Mazelyn: a bowl made of maplewood.

403. **that is so trye:** that is so excellent.

404. **his white leere:** properly speaking, flesh or skin. A.S. 'līra,' used here for the tightly-fitting linen garment.

405. **clooth of lake:** a fine white linen cloth; the name probably comes from the Dutch 'laken,' a cloth or sheet.

407. **an Aketon:** a short sleeveless tunic, worn under the hauberk.

408. **haubergeon:** a hauberk or coat of mail.

409. **ffor percynge of his herte:** to guard against piercing of his heart.

413. **cote Armour:** a sleeveless coat resembling a herald's tabard which was worn over the armour and usually made of silk or of some other fine material. The knight's 'coat-of-arms' was embroidered upon it and hence the 'coat-armour' served the purpose of identification. In *The Knight's Tale* Palamon and Arcite are recognised by means of it:

> 'But by hir cote-armoures and by hir gere
> The heraudes knew hem best in special.'

415: **wol debate:** will fight or quarrel.

419. **on ale and breed:** in mockery of the oath by the sacrament which was, of course, by 'bread and wine.'

421. **Bityde what bityde:** whatever might betide nothing should save the giant from his fate.

422. **Iambeux:** leggings or armour for the leg. Fr. 'jambe.'

quyrboilly: boiled leather. Fr. 'cuir bouilli'; it was leather soaked in hot water to soften it and then bent to any required shape.

424. **laton:** a mixed metal, containing copper and zinc.

425. **Rewel boon:** probably walrus ivory; the walrus was known in A.S. as the 'hors-hwæl' (i.e. horse-whale), and 'rewel' may be a corruption of 'hwæl'; walrus ivory was of very common use in the north.

430. **ful sharpe ygrounde:** a sharp point was ground on the spear; it was the custom to grind such a point immediately before a battle or tournament.

435. **heere is a fit:** a division or portion of the poem.

437. **wol I fonde:** I will try my best.

442. **ladyes love drury:** affection. Fr. 'drurie,' 'druerie,' love, passion.

444. **Romances of prys:** interesting romances.

445. **Hornchild:** the English romance so-called telling the love-story of Horn and the maiden Rimnild.

Ypotys: a kind of saint-legend; Ypotys was a youth miraculously sent to the emperor Adrian to instruct him in the Christian faith.

446. **Beves and of sir Gy:** the tales of Sir Bevis of Southampton and Sir Guy of Warwick, two of the most famous of local legends.

447. **sir lybeux:** the tale of Li Biaus Desconneus or the Fair Unknown, a French romance.

pleyn damour: plein d'amour, full of love. Judging from the name this must have been French also, but it is unknown.

455. **fro shonde:** from shame. A.S. 'scand,' disgrace.

456. **Auntrous:** adventurous.

458. **liggen:** to lie. A.S. 'licgan,' to lie.

459. **wonger:** pillow.

460. **dextrer:** war-horse, so-called because the squire was accustomed to lead it in his right hand.

464. **worthy under wede:** a noble knight; literally, 'noble in his garments.' A.S. 'wǣd,' dress or clothes.

470. **drasty speche:** filthy speech.

471. **I biteche:** I commit.

473. **lette me:** hinder me.

480. **aught in geeste:** a narrative poem.

483. **pyne:** torment or suffering.

486. **to daungerous:** too difficult to please.

489. **yow devyse:** explain to you.

492. **his felawe:** his fellow, i.e. the other Evangelists.

493. **hir sentence:** their meaning.

GLOSSARY

abyen: pay for.

agast: aghast, terrified or afraid.

aketoun: quilted tunic, to wear under the armour and keep its pressure from the body.

alday: always, continually.

ambil: amble, an ambling pace.

antiphoner: song-book, containing both words and music.

apayd: pleased, contented; yvele apayd, ill-pleased.

artow: art thou.

auntrous: adventurous.

auter: altar.

benygnytee: benignity, graciousness.

bisy: active, anxious.

boote: remedy, medicine.

certes: certainly.

cetewale: setwall, zedoary; an aromatic plant from the East Indies, used in medicine.

cheere: countenance, expression.

childhede: childhood.

cleere: bright, beautiful.

clergeon: a chorister.

clowe-gylofre: clove. Fr. 'clou de girofle.'

cordewane: Cordova leather.

cote-armour: a coat, usually of silk or linen, worn over the armour.

covent: convent.

daliance: dooth he daliance: jest with, make game with.

debate: fight, quarrel: either noun or verb.

despyt: despite.

dextrer: war-horse, so-called because the squire was accustomed to lead it with his right hand.

doghty: valiant, brave.

downe: hill, mountain. A.S. 'dūn.'

echon: each one.

elvyssh: elf-like, fairy-like.

entente: attention, i.e. heart.

felawe: fellow, companion.

ferther: further.

fit: a division of a poem. A.S. 'fitt,' song, poem.

fonde: attempt. A.S. 'fandian,' to try.

forby: by or past.

forlete: to leave. A.S. 'forlǣtan,' to leave behind.

frayneth: enquires. A.S. 'frignan,' to learn by asking.

fre: generous.

geestours: tellers of tales, reciters.

gent: gentle, accomplished.

goore: the spear-shaped piece of cloth in the side of a garment, hence the garment itself. A.S. 'gār,' javelin or spear.

goost: spirit, Holy Ghost. A.S. 'gāst,' spirit.

gruf: grovelling, flat on the ground.

halse: entreat or beseech. A.S. 'hālsian,' exorcise.

haubergeon: corslet.

haunt: dwelling-place.

heepe: heap or number. A.S. 'hĕap,' troop or band.

heng: hanged.

hente (hym): seized upon him. A.S. 'hentan,' to pursue.

hepe: hip.

herreth: praises. A.S. 'herian,' to praise.

heryinge: praising.

homward: on the way home.

homycide: man-slayer.

honest: honourable.

humblesse: humility.

hym lest: pleases him.

inwith: within.

jambeux: leggings. Fr. 'jambe,' leg.

jane: small silver coin; coin of Genoa.

japen: to jest.

Jewerye: Jews' quarter, Ghetto.

kan: know.

knowes: knees. A.S. 'cnĕow,' knee.

konnyng: cunning, skill, cleverness.

koude: knew.

kynde: nature. A.S. 'gecynd,' kind or nature.

laton: a mixed metal, brass.

laude: praise.

launcegay: lance.

leere: skin or close-fitting coat. A.S. 'līra,' flesh.

leet: let, cause.

lemman: lady-love.

lighte: illuminated, enlightened.

listeth: listen, imperat.plural.

love-drury: suffering for love, courtship.

make: mate. A.S. 'gemaca,' mate.

mawe: stomach.

mazelyn: bowl of maple-wood.

mede: mead, the drink made with honey.

merciable: merciful.

moot: must.

moyste: new.

ner: nearer.

oftaken: taken away.

Olifaunt: elephant.

papejay: popinjay, green woodpecker.

paramour: by love or for the sake of love.

parfourned: performed.

payndemayn: fine white bread, Panis Dominus.

place: chief house.

plat: flat.

popet: puppet, doll.

pricketh: rides or spurs.

privee: secret.

prymer: first reading-book.

quyrboilly: boiled leather, 'cuir bouilli,' leather

softened in hot water and bent to the required shape.

raughte: reached.
ravysedest: didst ravish.
rewel-boon: whalebone (or walrus ivory). A.S. 'hwæl-bān.'
rode: complexion, ruddy colour.
rote (by): by heart.
roune: whisper. A.S. 'rūnian,' whisper or mutter.

sapience: wisdom.
science: knowledge.
scoleward: on the way to school.
sely: innocent, happy. A.S. 'sǣlig,' blessed.
sentence: meaning.
shent: scolded.
shonde: shame. A.S. 'scand.'
solas: solace, comfort or pleasure.
sowded: united to, joined.
spelle: narrative or story.
spreynd: sprinkled.
stant: standeth, stands.
sterve: to die.
swal: swelled.
swayn: man, countryman. A.S. 'swān.'
syklatoun: fine, silken material, scarlet in colour.
symphonye: tabor.

Termagaunt: Trivigante, Diana in her three forms; generally used as meaning a heathen idol.
texpounden: to expound, to explain.
thee: to thrive. A.S. 'þēon;' to thrive.
thilke: the same.
thymage: the image.
trye: excellent.

unnethe, unnethes: scarcely. A.S. 'unēaþe.'
unstable: unfixed, wavering.
upright: full length, horizontal.

verrayment: truly. Fr. 'vraiment.'
vileynye: evil or bad. Fr. 'villein.'

wardrobe: a privy.
wende: turn or go.
wiste: knew.
wonger: pillow. A.S. 'wangere,' pillow.
wood: mad. A.S. 'wōd.'
woon: dwelling-place.
worth: got upon. A.S. 'weorþan.'
worthynesse: honour, dignity.

yborn: born.
ybounde: bound.
ykorven: carved.
ysprad: spread.
ytake: taken.
ytaught: taught.
ywis: certainly. A.S. 'gewiss.'